# BRAZIL

## MICHAEL'S GUIDE SERIES INCLUDES:

MICHAEL'S GUIDE ARGENTINA, CHILE, PARAGUAY
        & URUGUAY
MICHAEL'S GUIDE BOLIVIA & PERU
MICHAEL'S GUIDE ECUADOR, COLOMBIA & VENEZUELA
MICHAEL'S GUIDE BRAZIL
MICHAEL'S GUIDE SOUTH AMERICA (Continental)

MICHAEL'S GUIDE NORTHERN CALIFORNIA
MICHAEL'S GUIDE SOUTHERN CALIFORNIA
MICHAEL'S GUIDE CALIFORNIA

MICHAEL'S GUIDE SCANDINAVIA
MICHAEL'S GUIDE SCOTLAND
MICHAEL'S GUIDE SWITZERLAND
MICHAEL'S GUIDE HUNGARY
MICHAEL'S GUIDE TURKEY
MICHAEL'S GUIDE CYPRUS

MICHAEL'S GUIDE NEW YORK CITY
MICHAEL'S GUIDE LONDON
MICHAEL'S GUIDE PARIS
MICHAEL'S GUIDE AMSTERDAM
MICHAEL'S GUIDE BRUSSELS & ANTWERP
MICHAEL'S GUIDE FRANKFURT
MICHAEL'S GUIDE ROME
MICHAEL'S GUIDE MADRID
MICHAEL'S GUIDE BARCELONA
MICHAEL'S GUIDE JERUSALEM
MICHAEL'S GUIDE SEVILLE

# MICHAEL'S GUIDE

# BRAZIL

Series editor
Michael Shichor

*I* NBAL
Travel Information Ltd.

Inbal Travel Information Ltd.
P.O.Box 39090 Tel Aviv Israel 61390

©1993 edition
All rights reserved

**Intl. ISBN 965-288-082-5**

**Distributed in the United Kingdom by:**
Kuperard (London) Ltd.
9, Hampstead West
224 Iverson Road
West Hampstead
London NW6 2HL

**U.K. ISBN 1-85733-033-1**

# *C*ONTENTS

# *I* NTRODUCTION     15

# *B* RAZIL     53

# *I* NDEX

# *N* OTES

# *T*ABLE OF MAPS

# Preface

Until a few decades ago, Brazil was considered to be one of the most remote and forsaken countries in the world. Legends and stories about this country fired the imagination of writers, poets and dreamers: it was portrayed as a country of primeval jungles, pristine beaches and wild samba rhythms. A visit here was only for brave adventurers.

Today, however, the situation is different. Brazil has been moving forward with tremendous momentum, as reflected in great social and economic development and increasing westernization. Visitors to Brazil today will find some of the biggest and most modern metropolitan centers in the world, enchanting new holiday spots, along with charming colonial towns, fishing villages and remote jungles. Improved air connections to Brazil, as well as within the country, has made it an accessible destination, and millions of tourists from all over the world are attracted annually to this beautiful and fascinating country.

In writing this guide, we have aimed at coming out with a comprehensive, in-depth companion to the tourist who wants to get to know Brazil in a direct and personal way. People who travel to Brazil come from a variety of places and go for a variety of reasons, each with his or her own travelling style and on different schedules and budgets. An attempt has been made to create an information pool, which would combine material relevant to understanding the what, while contributing to the practicalities of the how.

While writing the guide with special emphasis on enlarging upon and clarifying general areas, we have not done so at the expense of the plethora of practical details which are of vital import, if you are to fully succeed in your venture and truly enjoy the experiences awaiting you.

Aware of the responsibility involved in being guide and companion to all who choose to see Brazil "through our looking glass", we have tried to compile as many facts and details as possible. From this pool of information, let each person take what fits best, what is most appropriate. This guide includes a vast selection of data, suitable for all tastes. Therefore, feel free to "browse" through the material offered and choose those topics which interest you and which contribute most to your travelling style.

In the course of this work, we have labored to separate the

wheat from the chaff and have tried to be as precise as possible. Naturally, many of the impressions and recommendations included in the guide are subjective, and reflect our personal tastes and preferences. However, we feel certain that they do contain those elements which will fulfill the expectations of the kind of tourist mentioned, and will guide and assist you in making the most of your trip, in as enjoyable, comprehensive and pleasant a way as possible.

Michael Shichor

## Using this Guide

In order to use this Guide in the most efficient way, we recommend that you read the following advice and act upon it.

The Guide includes a great deal of data meant to help you find your way and ensure that you see as much as possible with maximum saving of time, money and effort.

Before setting out, read the Introduction in its entirety. It provides the essential information you will need to know and understand before making the advance arrangements for your trip. Reviewing the material thoroughly, and acting upon it, means that you will be better organized and prepared for your trip.

The basic guideline in all of "MICHAEL'S GUIDE" publications is to survey places primarily in geographical sequence and not a thematic one. A geographical plan not only ensures the most efficient use of time, but also contributes dramatically to getting to know an area in its different aspects and acquiring a feel for it. Furthermore, you will be directed from a museum to a recommended restaurant or entertainment place, incorporating in your visit to one site several other locations which you may not have thought or heard of beforehand.

The chapters on main cities include maps and indexes of sites that will help you find out your way. On reaching each city, the Guide will direct you to recommended acommodation and restaurants. The maps will assist you in getting from one place to another.

There is a detailed index of all the places and sites covered in the Guide, at the end of the book.

At press time, information contained in this Guide was correct, but it is possible that you may discover certain inaccuracies due to unforeseen changes, and for that we apologise.

It is crucial that you check local information as much as possible when you actually arrive in Brazil. A good source of information is your hotel reception or local tourist board information office. Most towns have an information office open during the summer season.

In order to keep ourselves updated, we are in need of your help. The cooperation of those who enjoyed what this Guide has to offer is essential, and ensures that those who follow you, will have as much accurate information at their disposal as you did. For this purpose we have included a short questionnaire at the end and would be grateful, if you were to answer in and return it to us.

Have a good and enjoyable trip!

# *I*NTRODUCTION

A mere snatch of music instantly conveys the underlying magic and rhythm of Brazil, the largest country in South America. Brazilian music, the catchy Samba rhythm, and the national exhilaration of the annual carnival week are famous world over. The beauty of the Brazilian girls in their colorful costumes as they stroll down the streets of Rio de Janeiro, the wonders of the Copacabana beach, the famous Sugarloaf Mountain and the Corcovado are not easily forgotten.

Once a remote Portuguese colony in the New World, Brazil is today an important member of the international community, and a pillar of the Third World. A tangle of economic, political, social, and geographic problems prevent Brazil from real development and advancement. The tremendous potential is there, and if it is used wisely Brazil could have a brilliant future, where her beauty, her charm, and her social and economic potential will at last find full expression.

This vast and beautiful country offers the tourist a number of options: living it up in Rio de Janeiro, a turbulent cruise along the Amazon tributaries, a visit to the colonial town of Ouro-Preto or to the city of tommorrow — Brasília. Brazil is a captivating country, one that is open, friendly, and unique.

# *I**NTRODUCTION*

## Part One — Getting to know Brazil

### History

Towards the end of the 15th century, when new sea routes and continents — which were to change the face of the world — were being discovered, Portuguese navigators were attempting to find a route to India and the Far East. While the Spanish navigators were sailing west to what was later called America — the Portuguese sailed south along the African coast. In 1487 they reached the Cape of Good Hope, and ten years later the Far East.

In 1494, just two years after Columbus' momentous discovery, Spain and Portugal signed the Treaty of Tordesillas, an agreement instated by the Spanish rulers through which the Pope granted them the newly discovered territories to the west of an imaginary line drawn from the north to the south; all that lay east belonged to Portugal, providing this kingdom the basis for sovereignty over Brazil, which, incidentally, was not discovered for another six years. In 1500 the Spanish landed in Brazil, but did not stay. That same year, the Portuguese navigator Pedro Alvares Cabral's expedition landed on the coast of Bahia in northeast Brazil, and claimed the territory for the Portuguese crown. Unlike the Spanish, who encountered the rich and sophisticated cultures of the Aztecs and Incas, the Portuguese found only semi-nomadic Indian tribes subsisting off a primitive agriculture. These Indians lived in small and isolated communities and were extremely hostile towards the newcomers.

From an economic point of view, the newly discovered country was also somewhat disappointing. The only natural resource that could be exploited was the "coal tree" — *pau brasil* in Portuguese — which gave Brazil its name. The Portuguese were therefore in no hurry to expand settlement here, preferring to further their trade links with the rich markets of the Far East.

Only in 1530 did the first colonizing expedition reach Brazil, bringing the animals, seeds, and agricultural equipment needed to set up a permanent settlement. One after another, small coastal towns sprang up — initially in the São Vicente region (now the state of São Paulo), and later in the north, in the area of Salvador. Fear of Indian tribes prevented the colonials from penetrating inland. They settled mainly along the coastal strip between Bahia in the north and Porto-Alegre in the south. As the settlements grew, mainly during the 16th and 17th centuries, a new administrative policy was adopted to ensure control of the territory. The coastal strip was divided into administrative districts — *capitanias* — headed by powerful governors who were responsible for defending and developing their region.

Since the middle of the 16th century, the combination of the growing European demand for sugar, Portuguese navigational initiative, and the fertile lands of northeast Brazil (what is today the Pernambuco region) gave much impetus to settlement. Brazil became the world's largest sugar producer. The extensive sugar plantations were worked mainly by black slaves imported from Africa, who laid the foundations for Brazil's unique ethnic structure.

In 1580, Philip II of Spain assumed the Portuguese crown and claimed the country for Spain. For 60 years, the two Iberian kingdoms were a single state. This situation had far-reaching repercussions on Brazil. The merger in practice nullified the Tordesillas agreement, making it possible for the Portuguese to settle further inland. At the same time, Spain, and consequently Brazil too, became involved in a 30-year war with Holland. The Dutch conquered large portions of northeast Brazil, where sugar — the prime economic resource — was grown. The westward extension of settlement laid the foundations for Brazil's immense size, since the Portuguese refused to yield the territories they had settled during the years of union, and expelled the Dutch in 1654.

Perhaps the most important outcome of inland settlement was the discovery of gold, and later diamonds. In the 18th century, colonial expeditions, called *bandeirantes*, sent north and west from São Paulo, discovered significant amounts of gold in what is today the state of Minas Gerais. This led to a gold rush similar to the one in the United States. Thousands left the coastal towns, and masses of immigrants arrived from Portugal and other parts of Europe, flocking to the mining towns that sprouted in the new regions. Agricultural settlements grew alongside them to provide for their needs. In a matter of decades Brazil was transformed from a remote and isolated corner of the world to a magnet for immigration, and a popular center that was developing at a galloping pace, and whose future was full of hope.

As the gold fever subsided and diamond export waned, tranquility returned to the country, and practicality replaced dreams. Coffee production soon overshadowed gold production as Brazil began cultivating top-grade coffee, first near Rio de Janeiro, and subsequently in the south near São Paulo and Porto Alegre. Because of a suitable climate, soil, and elevation, Brazil produces coffee beans of choice quality. Since the second half of the 19th century, coffee has been one of the most important components of Brazilian economy, and the country's most important export.

The frequent changes and accelerated development also brought about administrative and constitutional changes. At the end of the 18th century, equal rights were granted to the Indians, liberal immigration laws were promulgated, and Rio de Janeiro replaced Salvador as the country's capital. This was due to its command of the main routes to Minas Gerais, with its rich mines, and because of its proximity to the growing settlements in the south.

The desire for independence was already apparent at the start of the 18th century. Growing dissatisfaction was felt since Portugal effectively controlled Brazilian commerce, dictating its scope, terms, and profits. Toward the end of the century, under the influence of the events in North America and the ideals of the French Revolution, ideas of independence began to take shape, and insurrections occurred in several areas. Freedom was in the air, just as in Europe and other Latin American countries. It was largely promoted by a new intellectual elite, which exploited the economic crisis, in particular the decline of gold and sugar exports, to further their ends. One of the rebel leaders of the period was Tiradentes, who is famous for his uncompromising stance in favor of ridding Brazil of the Portuguese crown. To this day he is a symbol of freedom and independence for Brazilians.

Unlike its neighbors which gained independence only after long and bloody battles, Brazil followed a gradual and moderate course, and managed to avoid armed confrontation. In 1808 Napoleon conquered Portugal. The Portuguese royal family fled Lisbon for Brazil, making it the seat of the monarchy, and they were welcomed with open arms. In 1815, Brazil was declared an independent state, federated with the mother country and subject to the Portuguese crown. Its ports were opened to free, large-scale trade. In 1821, the king returned to Portugal, where he vainly attempted to rescind some of the progressive economic and political concessions he had granted Brazil. His son, Dom Pedro I, joined forces with the secessionists. In 1822, when Brazil's independence was declared, he was chosen as its first Emperor.

Dom Pedro wanted to establish absolute monarchy, and tried to dissolve parliament. The parliament, on the other hand, tried to establish a liberal new constitution, but this resistance was met with force. On his father's death in 1826, Dom Pedro inherited the Portuguese crown. A short while later, he abdicated in favor his young daughter, Maria de Gloria, who became Queen Gloria II of Portugal. In 1831, unable to come to an agreement with the Brazilian parliament, Dom Pedro abdicated the Brazilian throne as well, in favor of his young son, Dom Pedro II.

The period under the leadership of Dom Pedro II was far more tranquil. Internal affairs stabilized, substantial resources were channeled into development, many immigrants were absorbed from Europe, and Brazil embarked on an era of prosperity. Dom Pedro II ruled for 49 years, during which time he laid much of the foundations of modern Brazil. Dom Pedro improved the bureaucracy, expanded education, health, and welfare services, and advanced international trade and commerce. His liberal policies, the most significant being the abolition of slavery and the emancipation of 700,000 black slaves in 1888, were strongly opposed by the landowners and the wealthy. In 1889 they banded together under the leadership of Marshal Fonesca, deposed Dom Pedro, and declared a republic.

At that time, northern Brazil was enjoying unprecedented prosperity. The discovery of the rubber tree in the Amazon region, and the eagerness with which this product was greeted in Europe, led to an extraordinary economic boom, which helped create a moderate political climate. Brazil's central government adopted liberal and conciliatory social and international policies, and with the help of one of Brazil's greatest leaders ever, the Baron Rio Branco, the country signed border agreements with its neighbors.

Brazil supported the Allies against Germany in both World Wars, winning it great sympathy in the West. The liberal government continued, but the economic crisis of the late 1920s brought about unpleasant political changes. The most important of these was the end of the "first republic" and the inauguration of the second, when, for the first time in its history, Brazil suffered a violent revolution. In 1930, a group of rebels led by Getulio Vargas, seized power and continued to rule Brazil for fifteen successive years. Vargas' first step was to alter the system by which the president was elected. Formerly, electors had chosen the president under the direction of the powerful state governors. The strong opposition that initially greeted his rule slowly diminished. In 1934 Vargas drew up a new constitution by which, among other things, women were granted the franchise. In 1937, a short while before the presidential elections, the internal climate grew so heated that Vargas declared a state of emergency. He dissolved Congress, and concentrated most power into his own hands.

During his rule, Vargas instituted a number of far-reaching reforms in education and welfare. He narrowed the social gap, and developed the western sector of Brazil, which was virtually uninhabited till then. In the early 1940s, Vargas restored some civil liberties, and allowed the formation of political parties. In 1945, in the face of mounting opposition to his rule, he resigned.

General Dutra, Minister of Defense under Vargas, won the presidency in the ensuing democratic elections. Dutra drew up a new constitution safeguarding individual liberties. In 1951, Vargas was re-elected president, but his rule was beset with serious economic problems and heavy pressure from the opposition.

In 1954, Vargas committed suicide under scandalous circumstances, following the attempted murder of one of the leaders of the opposition. The new president, Juscelino Kubitschek, led the country into a period of slow but steady economic growth, continued the policy of settling the west, and laid the foundations of Brazil's glorious new capital — Brasília.

Brazil's economic development led to galloping inflation and social unrest in the industrial cities. The 1960s began in political and economic chaos. An economic austerity policy was instituted, but this too failed. In April 1964, in an extraordinary move, the Congress elected a military man, General Castelo Branco, as president, with a mandate to stabilize the economy and social conditions.

For 20 years, a military junta ruled Brazil, suppressing opposition and restricting freedom of expression and association. Concurrently, attempts were made to develop the economy, agrarian reforms were instituted, power stations were set up, and unprecedentedly large amounts of foreign capital were raised. But these measures failed to alleviate the economic situation. The foreign debt grew to such enormous proportions that it was doubtful if it could ever be paid off, inflation surpassed government control, and a food shortage threatened to lead to a violent uprising on the part of the socially deprived.

In 1984, the army gave in to popular opinion, and new elections were held. The victor, Tancredo Neves from the state of Minas Gerais, coined the slogan *Nova Republica* ("the new republic"), which would avoid showy but economically unsound projects, make a concerted effort to solve problems of unemployment, housing, nutrition, and agricultural settlement, restore civil rights, and put an end to oppression. Neves (or Tancredo, as he was known by the masses) gained mass approval and public support for his program. But Tancredo, who had won the elections by a large majority, never reached the presidential residence,

Planalto, in Brasília. A fatal illness struck him a few days before the scheduled inauguration. His deputy, Jose Sarney, was sworn into office in his stead.

The day Tancredo died was a bitter day to all Brazilians. Hundreds of thousands of mourners participated in the funeral cortege as it made its way from São Paulo to Brasília. The procession ended at his birthplace in Minas Gerais. Sarney, his deputy, took over the presidency, and assumed the task of leadership under extremely difficult conditions. He had strong public support both at home and abroad, and his presidency has marked an economic, social, and political turning point. Under Sarney's leadership faith in political and public establishment was restored, but the economic instability and the huge external debt appear to be a chronical disease. So is the corruption in government. In 1992, President Colhor de Mello was involved in such a scandal, what brought to Brazil a political earthquake.

In June 1992 the "Earth Summit", the first international convention in history concerning the global ecological problems took place in Rio de Janeiro. In this act Brazil has put itself at the front of the fight for a better, less poluted, world.

## Geography and climate

Brazil has an area of 8,514,000 sq/km, which is half the area of the entire South American continent and as large as the whole of Europe. It is the fifth largest country in the world. Brazil's border stretches for some 15,720 km, 7408 km of them along the Atlantic coast. Brazil borders on every South American country, except Chile and Ecuador.

Brazil is a federal republic, consisting of 24 states and two territories. The equator transverses the north of the country. Although about 90% of Brazil is located in the tropics, its climate modified by the high altitude. Most of Brazil lies, 500-1000 meters above sea level. North Brazil, or *Amazonia*, is covered in thick forest, while the center is mainly savanna land, with sparse, low vegetation.

Most of the plateau consists of extremely ancient granite rock, which has been eroded and leveled over the last 700 million years. The plateau is bordered by the Andes in the west, by the Amazon basin in the north, and by the coastal mountain range in the east. The huge Amazon basin, the largest river-basin in the world, is a vast plain of silt washed down from the Andes, and covered in thick forest. The mountains, on the other hand, are extremely steep, with peaks right on the coast. These steep mountains make inland Brazil virtually inaccessible, and explain why settlement is concentrated along the coast.

# *I*NTRODUCTION

The Brazilian plateau is drained by three main rivers: the Amazon in the north, the São Francisco in the center, and the Parana.

In terms of settlement, Brazil can be divided into five main areas, each with its own topography and climate.

**Amazonia:** The largest and most unique area of Brazil is its northern sector. Amazonia stretches over 60% of Brazil's area, but is home to only 4% of the country's population. The climate is tropical — hot and humid — with a high precipitation rate (more than 2000 mm of rainfall annually) and due to its proximity to the equator, there is little seasonal variation and the temperature is constant the year round.

Amazonia is covered in dense forest, which comprises a third of the world's natural forests. A thousand species of trees and plants grow in it, and about 2000 species of fish and aquatic animals inhabit its rivers. Over the last decades, considerable effort has been put into developing the area, and particularly into exploiting its many mineral resources. Brazilian governments have done much to encourage settlement, build roads, and set up agricultural and industrial enterprises. Manaus, for example, was declared a free port, which led to a significant boom. Another huge government project was the Trans-Amazon highway. This project, which was intended to encourage settlement in the jungle, ended in bitter failure. Even though some parts of the road are still passable, most of this difficult route — which its planners saw as a true miracle of engineering — is neglected and overgrown by jungle vegetation. On the other hand, dozens of mining towns have mushroomed, full of fortune-hunters intent on discovering diamonds or other treasures in the area.

**The Northeast:** This area preserves remnants of its Spanish and Dutch colonial past. Many of the current population are descended from the Black slaves who worked the sugar plantations. Northeast Brazil is one of Brazil's least developed areas. Even though about one-third of the total population lives here, it has no real industrial or agricultural infrastructure. Over the last few years there has been a greater impetus toward development. The educational network has been expanded and a basis has been laid for improving the quality of life. In spite of this, the local inhabitants, in particular those who live far from the main towns of Bahia and Recife, still live in the primitive conditions of shameful poverty, gnawing hunger, and ignorance handed down by their ancestors. The weather is extremely fickle, sometimes dry almost to the point of drought, while in other seasons, awesome floods sweep away entire towns and villages.

**The Southeast:** This is Brazil's most developed, industrialized and populated area. Most of the country's economic activity takes place in the three cities of Rio de Janeiro, São Paulo, and Belo Horizonte. The reason for this is the pleasant climate in these areas — tropical to temperate — which enables the cultivation of top-grade agricultural products, and encourages settlement and broad industrial development. The area has many mineral resources, whose exploitation and sale has a major effect on the country's economy.

**The South:** The climate of southern Brazil is temperate in the main. The fertile plains are used as pastureland and for cultivation of a variety of crops. There is also some light industry here, and ports through which the local produce is exported. The south has always attracted European immigrants, who make their presence felt. Most Europeans here work in agriculture and live on farms or small rural settlements, living a lifestyle similar to the one they had in Europe.

**The West:** This is definitely Brazil's least-known or most "neglected" section. The huge states of Mato Grosso and Goias are almost entirely uninhabited. Only in recent years has public attention been directed to these places. Most of the land is savanna. In the heart of this area lies Brazil's new capital — Brasília — which, since it was built, has done much to assist this difficult and problematic region and give new hope to its inhabitants. The area has a hot climate and the precipitation increases as one goes further south.

## Population

Since Brazil covers half the South American continent, its population, currently estimated at about 160 million, correspondingly accounts for nearly half the total population of South America. The people are a mixture of various races, which accounts for Brazil's rich and diversified cultural life.

Brazil's population has grown at an astonishing rate since the beginning of the century, when the population was a mere 17 million. Only five million were Europeans (a third Portuguese, a third Italian, and the remaining third Spanish, German, etc.). The other 12 million were Blacks and Indians. During the 17th and 18th century, the Portuguese colonists "imported" millions of Black slaves, mainly from West Africa, to work the sugar plantations. These Blacks became an important demographic factor. They intermarried with the Portuguese, producing a distinctive ethnic group, whose social imprint is felt to this day.

Most immigration to Brazil took place in the 19th and 20th centuries, when millions of immigrants from all over the world landed on its shores. Most of the immigrants settled in the large cities and along the coastal strip. They began to intermarry, and the population grew rapidly. The Portuguese language and Catholicism are dominant. Some people see these as the main factors in overcoming ethnic and communal differences and creating the country's strong sense of unity (90% of Brazilians are Catholics, making Brazil the largest Catholic country in the world).

Nowadays, the population consists of about 60% Whites, over 20% *Mestizos* (mixed Portuguese and Indian) and *Mulattos* (mixed Portuguese and Blacks), 15% Blacks, and the remaining are Indians, Japanese, and other minorities. The Whites live mainly in south Brazil and along the coast. Most are "new" immigrants, having arrived since the second half of the 19th century. Only a few can trace their ancestry back to colonial roots. The Blacks are all descendants of the slaves who numbered an estimated 4-6 million at the end of the 19th century, when slavery was abolished. Large concentrations of Blacks can be found in Bahia, Rio, and Minas Gerais, the regions of sugar plantations, industrial development, and mines, where the slaves were employed. Only about 200,000 Indians survived. They are mainly to be found in remote areas of the Amazonia and Mato Grosso States. Many Indians perished from disease and the impact of modernization, while others were absorbed into the immigrant population, abandoning their traditional roots. FUNAI, the national authority that deals with all matters relating to the Indians, watches over the assimilation process and attempts to control their exposure to the modern world, thus making the transition less painful.

Immigration from the Far East has also played an important part in Brazilian society. About half a million Japanese live in Brazil, mostly in São Paulo. Their presence is felt in industry and commerce.

In spite of the complex racial mixture, there are no racial or sectarian conflicts. Everyone speaks Portuguese, and religion is a personal matter. Even though the vast majority are Catholics, a variety of pagan traditions and rites have been preserved, in particular African voodoo. These traditions flourish alongside the Church, and often Christian and pagan rites intermingle.

The population distribution is by no means uniform. Almost the entire population — 90% — lives along the Atlantic coast, and in the states of São Paulo and Minas Gerais. About 80% of the population live in urban environments. Government attempts to encourage settlement in the west and inland, which culminated in the building of Brasília in the center of the country, have had very limited success. The vast majority still prefer the cities, which are consequently expanding continually, without adequate urban planning. The consequences of uncontrolled urbanization are extremely painful. The most obvious are the slums, or *favelas* as they are known in Brazil, which surround almost every large city. Thousands of citizens live there in unhygienic, sub-human economic and social conditions. Poverty, distress, and the lack of job opportunities lead to crime, drug abuse, prostitution, and other blights and diseases. These have spread to sizable portions of Brazilian society, threatening to undermine its foundations.

To this is added the lack of Government policy concerning family planning. This leads to an extremely rapid population growth, at a rate of 2.5% per annum, i.e., an annual increase of three million. About half the total population are children, mostly of school age. In spite of untiring efforts, the government is unable to help all of them, and many children roam the streets. About a quarter of Brazil's population is thought to be illiterate.

## Government
The country is led by a president and vice president, who are elected for a six year term. The legislative bodies are the Senate, which has three representatives from each state, and the House of Representatives, with 280 members elected every four years on a proportional geographical basis. The president has broad powers and a virtually unrestricted say in all matters relating to legislation and decrees, although his use of these prerogatives is being restricted by the process of democratization. In 1985 the military regime came to an end, and the country was once again headed by a civilian president.

Each state of the federal republic has its own governor and legislature. They are responsible for internal affairs, administration, education, etc. The governor and members of the legislature are democratically elected on a party basis.

## Economy
Brazil's economy is based on agriculture and industry, including sophisticated hydroelectric plants and oil-drilling rigs. However, the country also has gigantic foreign debts, and is dependent on imported energy sources, and other products.

**Agriculture:** Basically, Brazil is agriculturally self sufficient. About one third of the population makes its living from agriculture, which not only satisfies local needs (except for wheat), but also provides about one third of the world's coffee.

Brazil is one of the world's largest agricultural states. In addition to its famous coffee production, it produces soya, cocoa, tobacco, cotton, sugar, and meat. The agricultural sector is growing year by year, particularly as a result of the expansion of agricultural training. This growth is impeded every so often by fluctuations on the world coffee market, which have a direct effect on the entire Brazilian economy.

Since agriculture accounts for about 50% of total export revenues, it is not surprising that successive governments have invested large resources in developing and diversifying it. Government bodies are continually attempting to modernize techniques, which in most parts of the country (particularly the northeast) are still fairly primitive, due to the low educational level of the inhabitants. Over the past twenty years, however, there have been considerable achievements in this area. Unlike the north, the south, especially the coffee growing areas, uses the most up-to-date agricultural technology.

Cattle ranching is a major industry in Brazil, with an estimated 200 million head of cattle. Meat is a central component of the national diet, and dairy products are also important. Most livestock is raised in the south, from which a considerable amount of meat is exported to Europe, the United States, and other countries.

Half of Brazil is covered with virgin forest, much of it carved up by rivers and streams. This restricts the amount of land that can be used for farming. However, the Brazilians have managed to put this ready-made forest to commercial use. The export of various kinds of wood is a growing industry.

**Minerals:** Brazil has been blessed with an abundance of mineral wealth. Iron, oil, magnesium, uranium, gold, and silver are just a few of the metals and minerals that lie buried in its soil. Their extraction is very important from both the economic and social points of view.

The discovery of gold, diamonds and other minerals had not only economic repercussions, but also social and demographic ones. Formerly, the state of Minas Gerais was the major mining area, but today it has been overshadowed by Amazonia. However, wherever the location, the phenomenon is the same. When a natural resource is discovered in commercial quantities, and the infrastructure for its extraction and marketing has been laid down, there is a marked increase in immigration to the area, and accelerated economic development.

The most serious problem in exploiting the mineral resources is their distance from ports and industrial centers. This makes the mining process more difficult and the product more expensive, so that the commercial potential is limited. However, iron, which

# *INTRODUCTION*

is found in plentiful supply in Minas Gerais and Amazonia, has in the last few decades become the mining industry's most important metal and the most significant raw material used in national industry. Iron mining laid the basis for Brazil's heavy industry, in particular the automobile and weapons industries. It is growing in importance every year.

**Industry:** The history of Brazilian industry is marked by ups and downs that are not always the result of commercial success or failure. In an attempt to develop local industry and avoid almost total dependence on agriculture, Brazil's various governments, virtually since the beginning of the 20th century, have given special consideration to the establishment of industrial enterprises. The basic idea was, and still is, to supply local consumption, i.e., to manufacture rather than import, and eventually to export. In the 1960's and the 1970's, Brazilian industry took a giant step forward, new factories were established, workers were trained, and production increased on an annual basis at an unprecedented rate world over. However, the masterminds of this boom neglected to lay a suitable infrastructure — in particular with regard to energy sources, the utilization of raw materials and the development of transport routes. As a result, a sharp recession ensued in the 1980s, economic growth slackened off considerably, and many industrial plants ran into financial difficulties, which repercutes in the 1990s economic infrastructure, widening the gap even more with the developed countries of the West.

Strict import restrictions limit competition from foreign products and assist domestic industry in the battle for the local market. Today, Brazil manufactures almost all its own cars, many electronic goods, petrochemical products, and weapons. Brazil is the fifth-largest arms manufacturer in the world.

Industrial exports are slowly catching up with agriculture's hitherto unquestioned supremacy, and nowadays the two are more or less on an equal footing.

**Energy:** Oil, mainly from the Middle East, accounts for roughly half of Brazil's total imports. About three-quarters of Brazil's total oil consumption is imported, which explains the sudden shift in national priorities toward the development of alternative energy sources, and the expansion of the local oil industry.

The government oil company Petrobras is investigating with admirable thoroughness, all potential oil sources in Amazonia and along the coast. They are expanding drilling and pumping operations in existing oil fields, in particular around Bahia and Campos, and investing huge sums in setting up oil refineries.

# *I*NTRODUCTION

At the same time special attention is being given to alternative energy sources. Many engines now run on alcohol instead of gasoline. This alcohol is obtained from sugar cane through a relatively inexpensive chemical process. Nuclear energy is also being considered, but its use is still rather limited.

The most important energy source after petroleum is hydroenergy, since water is so plentiful in Brazil. The huge hydroelectric plant at Itaipu, on the Paraguayan border, is the crowning glory of a series of similar plants, which already supply about 40% of all Brazil's energy, and about 90% of its electricity. Brazil is investing huge sums in developing hydroelectric energy in order to develop it into the country's main energy source, to free itself from its stifling dependence on oil.

Itaipu, a joint Brazilian-Paraguayan venture, is currently one of the largest hydroelectric plants in the world, its output is at some 12,000 megawatts. Twenty billion dollars have been invested in the project. The governments involved, view it not only as a very significant economic development, but also as a justifiable source of national pride.

**Transport and communication**: One of the most serious economic and social problems which has to be faced by a country as vast as Brazil is how to overcome natural obstacles and vast distances. As settlement penetrated deeper inland, the need arose to build roads and establish a convenient and efficient communications network. In the last decades Brazil has invested billions of dollars in this field, and thousands of kilometers of paved roads and dirt tracks are built every year. About 90% of passenger transportation is overland. Many travelers use the comfortable and convenient public transport services. All the large cities have modern bus stations, and streamlined buses run to all parts of the country.

One of Brazil's most controversial projects is the Trans-Amazonia Highway, which cost billions of dollars. The road was intended to promote settlement in Amazonia, but the plan — initially a source of national pride — failed miserably. The plan met with fierce opposition from the local Indians, thousands of whom fell victim to diseases spread by the road builders. Over the past years, all attempts to encourage use of the route have failed, and the ongoing maintenance costs far exceed its economic benefits. Nowadays, vast stretches of the road are neglected, and the encroaching forest is swiftly reclaiming its rights.

In the field of civil aviation, Brazil is advancing at a rapid pace. Nearly every city and town has its own airport, with flight links throughout the country. Scheduled airlines operate alongside private companies which fly to remote destinations that lack regular commercial service. In addition, light aircraft may be rented. This method of transport is essential in a country of such vast distances, and it is becoming increasingly popular.

Brazil's seaports have also been developing continuously. The country's 20 ports, along the Atlantic coast and the Amazon River, handle most of the import and export trade.

The telephone network, datalines, databases, and other technological innovations are developing fast — but not fast enough — in Brazil. More rapid progress is held back because of the huge investment required. In spite of this, Brazil has launched its own communications satellite, and is able to boast sophisticated computerized systems in both the private and public sectors.

**Conclusion**
At the turn of the century Brazil faces a severe economic crisis. Faulty planning has created a foreign debt of roughly one hundred billion dollars, the interest on which alone is sufficient to threaten the country's ability to survive. Add to this the cumulative trade deficit, difficulties in obtaining credit, and social problems that in any case make it impossible to apply a policy of restraint to the tottering economy. The government is consistently attempting to incorporate policies of fiscal restraint and to reduce the public sector's budget, at the recommendation of the International Monetary Fund, a fact many Brazilians dislike, not only because these measures undermine a social fabric already rent by the recession, but also because it is a way of giving up sovereignty. It is hard to foresee how Brazilian economy shall develop in the near future.

Rapid, unplanned urbanization without an economic base has increased the public pressure on the government. Unemployment is spreading and taking on a dangerous aspect in the absence of suitable mechanisms of unemployment compensation, supervision, and welfare. The disproportional distribution of incomes perpetuates a situation of social inequality, especially in the poorer regions of the country such as the northeast, where the average annual per capita income is a mere tenth of that in São Paulo.

# Language
Unlike the other Latin American countries, where Spanish is spoken, Brazil's national tongue is Portuguese; the heritage of the Portuguese colonizers. However, the Brazilian accent is totally different from that heard in Portugal. Moreover, within Brazil

itself, there are regional dialects. For example, the pronunciation and idioms of the south are quite different from those of the north, to such an extent that one Brazilian can easily identify where another comes from merely by his speech. English speakers will encounter the same problem as in the rest of South America: although English is spoken in all large cities, it is almost impossible to find anyone who speaks English in provincial towns and remote villages. So it is a good idea to try and master the basics of Portuguese before arriving in Brazil, or you will find it hard to make yourself understood.

Although the languages are different, Spanish speakers will probably learn Portuguese fast, at least enough to manage.

## Brazilian music

Music plays a major part in the life of Brazilians, and Brazilian music is extremely rich and varied. Who doesn't recognize the famous samba, which is one of the national symbols of Brazil? However, contrary to what is commonly believed, the streets do not resound with the strains of the samba from morning to night, except during the Carnival and other celebrations. On ordinary days, you can hear the samba only in clubs or at special events. The samba is popular mainly in southeast Brazil. In the north, other beats are more popular, such as the *forro* or *frevo*. These have a faster tempo, and the songs are accompanied on the accordion. The *bossa nova* is slower and more lyrical, and most popular among the bohemian section of society. Among the most famous composers and musicians of the bossa nova are Vinicius de Morais, Toquinho, Antonio Jobim, Dorival Caimi, and Chico Buarque.

Brazilian pop music has also won international acclaim. Some of Brazil's most famous pop singers are Gal Costa, Jorge Ben, and Gilberto Gil. The latter is particularly influenced by Jamaican *reggae* and African music. Caetano Veloso and Djavan are extremely popular in Brazil itself, as is Elba Ramalho, who specializes in northern music. Egberto Gismonti — the famous jazz musician — has also captured a wide audience.

The influence of western pop and rock is evident in Brazil. An ever increasing number of pop singers and rock groups are making their appearance in Brazil.

We have mentioned only a few outstanding names in Brazilian music. If you hear of a show featuring one of the better Brazilian musicians, make sure not to miss it. The music — and watching the audience's reaction — will give you an idea of the part music plays in the life of the Brazilians.

# *I*NTRODUCTION

## Part Two — Setting Out

## Making the decision to go

### Who's going

You may think that Brazil is a country exclusively for the young. Music, girls, beaches, adventurous jungle treks, and much more. And you will indeed come across many young travelers exploring the expanses of this huge country, burdened only with a backpack (they are known as *mochileros*, from *mochila*, which means backpack in the vernacular). They may spend months traveling. For many of them, Brazil is merely one stage in a long journey through the South American continent.

These youngsters manage to get around a lot on next to nothing, and usually have interesting and exciting experiences. But make no mistake! Brazil is not only for the young. Do not imagine that adults must make do with a calm, uneventful, European trip. In recent years the Brazilian government has discovered the immense economic potential of foreign tourism. Hotels of all standards are being built at an accelerated pace, the major cities are all equipped to cater for tourists from all over the world, and the internal transport system is sophisticated, comfortable, and reliable. Of course the more "solid" tourists will skip the charming small coastal villages — the haunt of "laid back" youth — where only the most basic tourist facilities exist. On the other hand, they will have ample opportunity to absorb Brazil's culture and ambience, visit beautiful sites and interesting museums, and enjoy — if young in spirit — all-night entertainment in the best Brazilian tradition.

Inspiring trips into the wilds are also within the scope of the older tourist, and not only of the adventurous young. Many travel agencies organize trips to the jungle and marshlands. These trips may not be particularly daring — but they are sure to be fascinating.

**Businessmen** have the good fortune of being able to combine work with pleasure when visiting Brazil, and can get to know various economic systems as well as the beauties of this tropical country. Business travelers will no doubt tend to concentrate on the major cities, where they will find superb tourist facilities and a wide range of restaurants and places of entertainment.

# *I*NTRODUCTION

The famous easy-going Brazilian attitude, which is almost a way of life in its own right, also has its effect on the world of business, although business is in fact conducted in an efficient and thorough manner.

**Women and girls** need have no qualms about traveling through Brazil. Except for a few places that we would not recommend for girls on their own, and except for the fact that women should not walk around alone late at night, there is no reason why they should not visit the country. Traveling in pairs helps solving these problems a great deal.

## How to go

Obviously the most convenient way of traveling is as part of an organized group. Many companies specialize in guiding tour groups through various parts of Brazil. These are generally fairly expensive. If you choose this option, you will be spared most difficulties and problems, but you will also have less personal contact with Brazilians, and will not be free to decide on your own schedule, route, etc. Bear in mind, however, that very few Brazilians speak English, so if you don't have at least a smattering of Portuguese you may find yourself in a tight spot, and will certainly need lots of patience.

There are many and varied group tours. If you are considering this form of travel, make a list of places you want to visit, and then check out the various companies and their prices. Trips that include the Rio Carnival are especially popular.

Another way of visiting the country is of course on a private, individual basis. Here you are the master of your own time, you can choose where you want to go, when you want to go, how long to spend in each place, how much you want to spend, etc. There is no greater freedom than a long trip with no planned route or timetable, so that you can travel around at will, doing exactly as you please. Alas! not many people can allow themselves this luxury.

A compromise between an organized group and an individual trip is the **package tour**. If you have concluded that you don't want to join an organized group, check with various travel agencies, which sometimes offer really cheap deals that, while they may restrict you as far as the calendar is concerned, are quite inexpensive.

**Backpacking** is popular among young people, both Brazilians and foreigners. Many of them set out to tour South America over a period of several months, and make their way across the continent from country to country and from site to site. Brazil usually plays a central role in such trips. In the course of their travels these young travelers usually pick up Portuguese, gain a direct acquaintance with the local population, and usually manage to see interesting places that not many tourists find their way to.

Backpacking is a cheap, easy, and pleasant way to travel. Backpackers (*mochileros*) usually find a warm welcome wherever they go. Backpackers of many different nationalities tend to meet up in various places and travel together, so that even if you set off alone you are likely to meet many fellow tourists and are not likely to suffer from loneliness. Many prefer to travel in pairs — if only to soften the shock of impact with a new and foreign country. There is an advantage in traveling in pairs as far as accommodation and transportation is concerned — it is easier and cheaper when there are two of you.

Backpacking is inexpensive, but because of the frequent fluctuations in the currency rates, it is hard to estimate how much it can cost. This form of travel has certain difficulties; you will not be using the most comfortable means of transportation, and the hostels are very modest. You will need more time, more energy, and much more patience, openness, and good humor.

**Establishment-type tourists** and businessmen, who have limited time at their disposal and wish to visit many places comfortably, can make the most of their trip by planning ahead and reserving hotel rooms and plane seats in advance. If you fall into this category, make a list of the places you most wish to see, and plan your schedule accordingly. Advance booking is not always essential, and of course it restricts your freedom. Throughout this volume we have indicated places, routes, and seasons where demand is high. If these places are included in your plans, get a reliable travel agent to make reservations for you before you leave home.

## How long to stay
Brazil is so large you'll need several months to get to know it. Many tourists choose to come for short periods: a week during the Carnival season, a weekend in Rio, or similar short visits. Tourists who travel within the country by air and tour intensively can see considerable portions of the country within 3 or 4 weeks. In this length of time you can get to know many of Brazil's cities and some of its countryside. If you have only a limited period at your disposal and wish to travel overland, concentrate on one part of the country only. In a short period it is impossible, and not worth trying, to get to know both the coastal region — in southern and northern Brazil — as well as the inland regions and the Amazon basin. The *mochileros* who spends months

traveling through the country will tell you that even three or four months is not long enough to get to know the country really well.

## When to come; national holidays

The weather in Brazil is very pleasant in the winter months, between May and September. During the summer, from October to April, it is very hot and rainy. It is easier to tour in the winter, but there are fewer events at that time. The Carnival takes place at the end of February, at the height of summer. This is also the vacation season, when the beaches are packed with young people taking their annual break from study or work. If you wish to tour Brazil extensively, try to come in winter, but if you are on a short vacation, a summer visit is recommended.

Businesses close for the following national holidays: January 1, the Carnival days (around Shrove Tuesday), Good Friday, April 21, May 1, Corpus Christi, September 7 (Independence Day), November 1, November 15 (the day the republic was declared), and Christmas.

## How much does it cost?

Brazil is no longer a prohibitively expensive destination, as it once was. More and more airlines have scheduled flights to Brazil from all over the world, and the keen competition among them has brought down the airfare to no more than that for flights of similar length in the rest of the world.

## How to get there

**By air:** Brazil has excellent air links with most parts of the world. The national airline *Varig* runs daily flights to Brazil from various places in the United States, Europe, and the Far East. Most international flights land in Rio de Janeiro or São Paulo, but some fly to Belem, Recife, and Manaus.

There are many flights each day from the major cities of Western Europe, both on *Varig* and the various European airlines. Varig and *British Caledonian* have weekly flights from London to Recife, via Lisbon. *Air France* has a direct flight from Paris. There are flights to Manaus from Miami and Mexico City; and to Belem from Miami, New York, Montevideo, and Buenos Aires.

There is also a frequent daily service from other South American countries to a number of Brazilian cities.

**By land:** Good highways lead to Brazil from Argentina and Uruguay. There is a regular bus service from Buenos Aires, Montevideo, Santiago (Chile) and Asuncion (Paraguay). From

# *INTRODUCTION*

Santa Cruz in Bolivia you can reach the Brazilian border on the so-called "Train of Death". There is irregular transportation from Venezuela to Buena Vista, and from there you can continue southward. Only a long and tiring cruise on tributaries of the Amazon will get you, from Colombia and Peru, to Manaus and Belem.

## First steps

Once you have decided how to travel and when, all that is left is to make the practical arrangements. The following section deals with this topic, and outlines what you should do in advance of your trip to make it as successful, easy, pleasant, and inexpensive as possible.

### Documents

Most foreigners require a visa, which can be obtained at any Brazilian consulate. The visa allows entry up to three months after date of issue; the actual entrance stamp on your passport is valid for a stay of three months from date of entry. A three-month extension can be obtained from the Immigration Bureau in any of the large cities. A tourist card must be filled out when you enter the country, and must always be kept with your passport thereafter. On entry to Brazil the authorities usually require a certificate of immunisation against yellow fever.

An international driver's license is valid in Brazil, but remember to attach your original license. A student card carries no great weight in Brazil, and will not usually confer any discount. Always carry identification papers (passport). Surprise checks by policemen are common occurrences, and the absence of ID can lead to harrassment and unpleasantness.

### Insurance

No tourist should leave home without adequate insurance. Theft and robbery in Latin America as a whole, and in Brazil in particular, are by no means rare, and if you have not taken out baggage insurance you are liable to suffer a financial loss as well as the inconvenience connected with being the victim of crime.

Even more important is health insurance. The costs of medical care and medicine are very high. Don't leave such vital matter to the vagaries of chance; spend the small amount of time and money required to take out health and baggage insurance before you go, hoping that in retrospect it will have been quite unnecessary.

# *INTRODUCTION*

## Finances
The most popular and convenient currency in South America, both for spending and exchanging, is the American dollar, which is recognized and welcomed everywhere, and can easily be changed in the large cities. Various European currencies, such as the pound sterling, Deutschmark, and French franc, are also accepted, but are less sought after.

If your trip is short, take cash; but if you're staying for a longer period buy travelers' checks, to be on the safe side. In any case take along a credit card, which is accepted in many places.

## Health
The Brazilian health services are far from satisfactory, with the exception of the major cities — Rio de Janeiro and São Paulo — which have modern hospitals and many clinics. In the villages and countryside there are only rudimentary health services, and you should refrain from availing yourself of them as much as possible.

Most of the serious diseases that were endemic to Brazil a few decades ago have been eliminated in all but the most remote jungle regions. However, malaria is still common in the Amazon basin and the Pantanal; if you are planning to travel to remote areas, you must take anti-malaria pills with you. The immigration authorities at the border will usually ask to see a certificate of immunization against yellow fever, which you should obtain before leaving home.

Gastrointestinal diseases are still extremely common in Brazil, due to poor sanitation and inadequate storage methods. Take into account that you are quite likely to suffer intestinal problems at some stage in your journey. So come equipped with suitable medicines, and do not hesitate to consult a doctor in serious cases. Jaundice is a common disease — and the later it is discovered the worse it can be. Many people choose to be immunized against jaundice, but this does not always work, since there are many strains of the disease.

By drinking only mineral water you will considerably reduce the risks of catching an intestinal bug. In the countryside always boil drinking water and purify it with chlorine tablets.

Mosquitoes and other insects are common in many places, especially in the jungle and marshlands. Take along a large quantity of mosquito repellent; and since in spite of these you will still get plenty of bites — also take along a soothing ointment.

The beaches in the northeast are infested with worms that penetrate under the skin *"bichos"*. In order to prevent infection, never walk barefoot on the beaches or in the adjoining villages. If you get infected despite these precautions, go to the local doctor, who will easily cure you of this problem.

If you suffer from chronic diseases or allergies, take along a first-aid kit. Even though remote towns have plenty of pharmacies, the sanitary conditions in which the medicines are stored are suspect, to put it mildly. Below is a short list of medicines and essential medical supplies:

pain-killers
antipyretics
anti-malaria tablets
chlorine tablets for purifying water
antibiotic ointment
disinfectants
gauze, adhesive tape, adhesive bandages
anti-histamines
medicines for chronic ailments or allergies

If you wear glasses, be sure to take along a spare pair, and your prescription as well.

A final word: never neglect even a slight wound. A scratch you could have safely ignored at home can easily get infected. Good advice is to make sure you get an anti-tethanos vaccine before you leave home.

## What to take
As a general rule, the less you take the better. The advantages of traveling light far outweigh the satisfaction of a few extra clothes — after all, you're going on a trip, not a fashion show. When all is said and done, a large portion of what you take never gets used in any case, and you quickly learn that most of what you took along was quite unnecessary.

Remember, whatever you need — you'll manage to find during the trip — even if not of the same type, model, or quality you are used to. During the trip you'll be picking up many souvenirs and presents, so you should really take along the bare necessities — but plenty of resourcefulness.

**Clothing** depends on your destination and the season. Businessmen must be smartly dressed, although a jacket and tie are not usually necessary. In the large cities, appropriate evening dress is customary for both men and women, and sportswear for young people and children. *Mochileros* will feel most comfortable in jeans and casual wear, although they should also take along more festive wear for events that require this.

# *I*NTRODUCTION

Lightweight and simple clothes are always appreciated, and are easy to wash and carry. Avoid taking elegant evening attire that requires careful transport and special care. It just isn't worth the effort.

I wouldn't suggest taking along more than one backpack or suitcase. These too should be at the most average in size. Baggage weighing more than 15 kg can be a real burden, and more than 20 kg can be even expensive. Many airlines are strict about the baggage limit, and travelers with overweight have to pay for it.

Comfortable walking shoes are perhaps the most important item. These are appropriate for any type of trip or travel. It is not an exaggeration to say that a bad pair of shoes can utterly ruin a trip. So make a point of getting good walking shoes and don't skimp.

## Camping Gear

If you plan on traveling for a long period through Brazil and the neighboring countries, you must carry your equipment — including camping gear — in a backpack. When purchasing camping gear, make sure that its quality matches your needs. Remember that you will be using it for months on end, and that cheap equipment, which may save you money initially, in the long run may prove more trouble than it's worth. Below is a description of essential equipment.

**Backpack:** This should be light, with an inner metal frame, and laces to tie on a sleeping bag, mattress, etc.

**Sleeping bag:** This should be appropriate to the region and season. For a long trip through different climatic zones, it's best to get a warm, down-filled sleeping bag. It's important to buy a sleeping bag of the best quality, well-sewn and with a reliable zipper. Sleeping bags come in different sizes; select one that fits you. The "mummy" design — wide at the shoulders and narrow at the feet — is recommended. It keeps in body heat and is lighter to carry. Synthetic sleeping bags are cheaper, but are much larger, bulkier, and heavier. Remember that you'll be carrying your sleeping bag on your back for weeks and months, and the bother is simply not worth the savings. On the other hand, take into account that a down sleeping bag has one big disadvantage — when it gets wet it loses its efficiency and some of its special properties, and can be uncomfortable to sleep in.

**Mattress:** In order to be slightly more comfortable on the rocky beds on which you will be spending many a night, a lightweight mattress is recommended — especially if you are taking a down sleeping bag. There are two common kinds of mattress: foam-rubber and inflatable (specially for camping). The latter is more expensive but more comfortable, and guarantees a good night's sleep — essential after a long day of hiking.

**Tent:** This should preferably be a two-person two-layer tent with a groundsheet. A one-person tent is simply not large enough, since you are hardly likely to remain alone on your travels. A two-layer tent provides better protection against the rain, keeps in the heat, and keeps out moisture.

**A camping stove:** Highly essential for treks in the wilds of nature, and most economical when staying in towns and settled areas. Throughout South America it is almost impossible to find gas cylinders for camping stoves, and where these do exist they are very expensive. Consequently a kerosene stove is preferable. The most common and most highly recommended are manufactured by the Swedish "Optimus" company and "Coleman". They are reliable, safe, and easy to carry and use. But remember to use them with extreme caution. Inflammable material can cause disasters if not handled properly.

**Dishes:** A few good dishes, preferably metal or plastic. Store food in plastic or cloth bags, since boxes and cans take up a lot of room in a backpack.

**A water bottle:** Take along a collapsible water bottle with a 10-liter capacity — essential for long treks.

**Miscellaneous:** Penknife, flashlight, rope, hammock.

Purchasing the equipment is one of the greatest expenses of a trip. So check and compare prices, and take your time before buying. I want to stress yet again, however, that on no account should quality be sacrificed for economy, since you are likely to suffer in the end. Also bear in mind that camping gear is extremely popular among the locals, and at the end of your trip you will have no problem in selling your equipment for not much less than what you paid for it originally.

The traditional centers for buying equipment are London and New York. These have the largest selection at the most attractive prices. London has many stores that sell camping equipment; one of the best is the *YHA* (Youth Hostel Association) shop at 14 Southampton Street (Tel: 836-8541). This huge store sells everything — from shoe laces to emergency dried food. A potential traveler can enter the shop empty-handed and emerge in a matter of hours with all the equipment necessary for a trip round the world. YHA members get a 10% discount on all purchases.

# *I*NTRODUCTION

In New York you can purchase equipment at any one of the hundreds of stores that deal in camping and sport equipment. The largest of these, *Parragon*, offers an inexhaustible range of products at prices that suit every pocket.

## Photography

One of the most enjoyable aspects of a trip is taking photographs. It is worth making your photographic preparations in advance, acquiring appropriate equipment, and learning at least the basics of how to use your camera.

Many tourists wander through South America with sophisticated and complicated photographic equipment. Brazil, like all the continent, is a photographer's paradise, fertile ground for expression and creativity. Those who are familiar with the secrets of the art will come equipped with several cameras, lenses, and a range of film.

If, however, you wish to commemorate your trip without lugging a mobile studio around with you, it is recommend to take one camera with three lenses: a standard lens (50mm), a wide-angle lens, and a telephoto lens. A good lens that combines all three functions is the 35-210 zoom. Buy good and reliable equipment, and remember to wrap it well and to insure it. Avoid taking fancy and expensive equipment, since it is likely to get knocked about on the way. Such equipment can also attract thieves. Film is expensive in most South American countries, and Brazil is no exception, so take along plenty of film, since you can always sell what you don't use. As a general rule, use ASA 64 film, which is suitable for almost every type of light and weather conditions you'll encounter in South America. ASA 400 film is also worth taking, since it is hard to find, and particularly expensive when available. If you have to buy photographic supplies in Brazil itself, do so only in the large cities, since elsewhere, not only is film hard to come by and exorbitantly priced, most of it is also likely to have long since past its expiration date.

In Brazil film is developed in various sorts of laboratories, and it's not always worth taking the risk. As a rule, it's better to develop films in the United States or Europe. In some locations, such as Rio de Janeiro and São Paulo, you can have your film developed with relative safety in Kodak laboratories. Slide film whose purchase price includes developing should be sent directly to the company laboratory, which will return it directly to your home address.

# *I*NTRODUCTION

## Part Three — Easing the Shock: Where Have We Landed?

### Accommodation

The development of the tourist industry has led to a considerable expansion in available accommodation. All the major cities have a very large selection of hotels, ranging from first-class luxury hotels to modest pensions, which are called *pousadas*. The smaller places, such as the northern coastal villages, the Amazon region, and remote interior regions of the country, are equipped only with primitive guest houses, often without hot water, and in some there are either beds or hammocks. Hotels are classified by stars, under the auspices of the Brazilian Tourist Office, *Embratur*. However, classification seems to be somewhat inconsistent, and you are apt to come across two hotels with the same number of stars that bear only the most superficial resemblance. A five star hotel in Salvador may be the equivalent of a mere three star hotel in Rio, and so on.

The hotels are, however, clean and well kept, and hotel staff usually polite and helpful. Generally, the growing awareness of the importance of tourism has brought about a real change in tourist services, and improvements are noticeable from one year to the next.

There is no shortage of inexpensive accommodation. Such places are not always clean, and often not in the most attractive surroundings. Carefully check such places before taking a room, and never leave valuables in your room. No one speaks English in these places, so come prepared with a smattering of Portuguese and plenty of resourcefulness.

The tourist with modest requirements can always find intermediate class hotels in the cities. Although these are much less expensive than luxury hotels, the actual differences between them are not so striking. In these establishments, the staff does not speak English, but patience and persistence will go a long way.

In the coastal villages of Bahia and north Brazil, rooms can be rented for next to nothing. In some of these places, you can sleep in a hammock for a nominal charge. The owners of these pensions are usually very friendly and pleasant.

## What to eat, where and when

Brazilian cuisine is extremely varied, and the local dishes differ from one place to the next. In the south, for example, the influence of nearby Argentina and Uruguay is felt: prime beef is the staple diet, and the *Rodízio* restaurants, which serve "all you can eat", are part of the local scenery and folklore. In the Amazon area, by contrast, meat is a rarity, and locals live on fruit, fish, and rice. Bahia in the northeast has exotic and unique cuisine. Here you can find exquisite concoctions of seafood, prepared according to the African traditions brought over by the Black slaves.

The most popular dish in the southeast is *feijoãda* — a stew based on black beans, cooked slowly with an assortment of meats, mainly beef and pork, and served over rice. Traditional Brazilian side dishes are rice and brown or black beans cooked in sauce, *feijão*, and a condiment known as *farofa*, made from dried and coarsely ground potatoes or yucca, is often sprinkled over foods.

Brazil has a rich assortment of fruits, especially tropical ones. Bananas, pineapples, mangos, and papayas are merely some of the choice fresh fruit you can find in abundance in the markets at ridiculously low prices, especially in northeast Brazil. On every street corner you will come across stands selling fruit juice: *suco* is a water based juice, and *vitamina* a milk based one. Brazilians prepare *suco* or *vitamina* from all fruits, even avocados. Sounds strange? Try it anyway — you may change your mind. Another drink is sugar cane juice, *caldo de cana*, prepared in large, complicated machines.

Brazil is also noted for its variety of alcoholic beverages. The south, especially the state of Rio Granda do Sul, is famous for its choice wines. Brazil also manufactures good, strong beer known as *cerveja*, which comes bottled, and a milder draft beer known as *chope*. The national beverage is *cachaça*. This is an extremely potent type of rum, made from sugar cane, and is usually an acquired taste. Easier to take is *caipirinha*, which is *cachaça* diluted with lemon juice, sugar, and ice.

Brazil's most famous drink, of course, is coffee. However, don't expect anything outstanding, since most of Brazil's choice coffee is exported. Only a few companies manufacture top quality coffee for local consumption. In most cases you will find acceptable coffee, but not much more than that. Coffee is a very popular beverage, and almost every restaurant, even the most modest, will bring you a *cafezinho*, a small cup of coffee, at the end of your meal — on the house.

Brazil's dairy industry is highly developed, and all supermarkets sell a variety of cheeses, yoghurts, and other dairy products. Restaurants, too, serve delicious ice cream, cakes, and confectionery.

As a general rule, the food in Brazil is excellent, and served in generous portions. The price of a meal at a modest restaurant is extremely reasonable. Even first class restaurants do not charge exorbitant prices. A meal at a fancy restaurant in Brazil costs no more than an average meal in Europe or the States. The cost of a meal in more popular establishments is correspondingly less.

Most restaurants serve local fare, as well as a selection of continental dishes, and portions are usually huge. Fixed-price meals are especially reasonable and one portion can easily satisfy two people.

The large cities have many restaurants, with a wide range of prices and cuisine, but the smaller towns have a more restricted, although perfectly adequate, selection. Inexpensive restaurants are known as *lanchonetes*, and serve fixed-price meals, *comercial*, which usually consist of meat with rice and *feijão*.

## Domestic transportation

Brazil has an excellent internal transportation network, both by air and overland. Air transport is highly developed due to the vast distances that have to be covered. The three major airlines, *Varig-Cruzeiro*, *VASP* and *Trans-Brasil* run frequent and reliable flights to all parts of the country. Service on internal flights is excellent, and even surpasses that in Europe and North America.

*Varig* offers tourists an Air Pass, permitting travel on 5 internal flights over 21 day for a mere $440 (a connection would not account). This arrangement is highly recommended, especially if one has little time and wants to visit several parts of the country. You will find this arrangement rediculously cheap comparing with the regular fair, especially if you plan to include a visit to the remote areas of the country, like the Amazon. The Air Pass must be purchased outside Brazil, but routes can be decided upon once you are in the country. During the summer, make advance reservations. This is not essential during the rest of the year.

Interurban bus service is also excellent. Brazil has dozens

of competing bus companies, with modern, comfortable, air conditioned buses. The largest of these are *Itapemirim* and *Penha*. Remember, though, that the vast distances can make journeys somewhat tedious. (For example, the bus ride from Rio to Salvador takes more than 30 hours!).

The bus terminals (*rodoviarias*) are located on the outskirts of the towns. In the large cities, these terminals are modern and spacious, but in the villages they are often nothing more than small, miserable holes in the wall.

For interurban travel, buy tickets at least a day in advance. Always ask the exact price and count your change. Ticket clerks are not among the most honest of Brazilians.

Trains operate on a few main routes, but trips by rail are less comfortable and longer than bus trips. The Curitiba-Paranagua route is recommended, more for the scenery than for the journey itself. The train service between Rio and São Paulo is relatively efficient.

Driving in Brazil is no easy matter. Except for south and east Brazil, there are almost no roads, and those that do exist suffer from natural inclemencies and erosion. There are plenty of rent-a-car companies — in almost every town — but the rates are extremely high. As for hitchhiking, the answer is an emphatic no. Before trying to save a nickel or two, remember the numerous cases of hitchhiking tourists who were robbed, assaulted, and even killed. In Brazil one has to be extra careful. Since public transportation is efficient, comfortable and reasonable, there is absolutely no justification for putting one's life in danger.

## Keeping in touch

Generally speaking, the Brazilian postal services are efficient. All major cities have many post offices, from which you can send letters and parcels. It is best to send things only by air mail, and even by air, mail is often delayed. Surface mail is much cheaper but far less reliable, and will reach its destination, if at all, only after several months.

## Currency exchange

The Brazilian unit of currency is the *cruzeiro*, which is divided into 100 *centavos*. The *cruzeiro* is an unstable currency and its value against the dollar is always changing. There are bills of 1000, 20,000, 50,000 and 100,000 *cruzeiros*.

Currency exchanges (*casas-de-cambio*) are shops that trade in foreign currency. They are plentiful in all of Brazil's major cities, and most change foreign currency at the black market rate. This is the quickest and best legal method of purchasing *cruzados*. Private moneychangers may offer a slightly higher rate, but the extra time and hassle are not worthwhile.

Money changers will swoop down on you at the airport, especially in the offices of the taxi companies. They will invent 1001 fanciful reasons why you should change your dollars with them... In town the banks are closed, the situation is difficult, the dollar's falling, and so on and so forth. Don't panic: you will always be able to change your dollars at a better rate than the one they offer.

When leaving major cities for the hinterlands, be sure to take along sufficient local currency, since in the provinces changing money may prove somewhat complicated, and the rate will be lower than in the major cities.

## Tourist services

In recent years, Brazil has become more aware of the enormous economic potential of foreign tourism. As a result, the tourist infrastructure is being developed and improved. This infrastructure consists of a large selection of hotels of varying standards, many on a par with those in western countries, a plethora of restaurants, and a large number of rent-a-car services. Fleets of special tourist taxis — more comfortable and spacious than the standard ones — await tourists at hotels and airports. Many private companies provide guided tours and a variety of trips.

Most airports and central bus stations have a left-luggage counter and an information desk. In the large cities, tourist information centers are spread throughout the town, and some even have a telephone information service that operates round the clock. The main bureaus can provide you with maps, brochures, and up-to-date information on hotels and restaurants, and will be delighted to help you make hotel reservations. Many localities publish weekly or monthly bulletins concerning special events, places of entertainment, and other information useful to the tourist. These bulletins are distributed free of charge in information bureaus and most hotels.

In the smaller towns, however, the information provided by the information bureaus, which are usually located at the bus terminal, is scanty and limited.

## Overland border crossings

If you plan to visit neighboring countries, you will encounter at the border check-points the normal border-crossing hassle.

Each border crossing has two check points, one for each country. Sometimes these are situated in walking distance of each other, or on the opposite banks of a river, and sometimes you may even have to travel a short stretch to get from one to the other. In any case, be sure to stop at both check points. At the first, your passport will be stamped with an exit visa. At the second, your passport will be stamped with an entry visa, and you'll also receive a tourist visa which is usually valid for a maximum of 90 days. Although you may extend the visa once you're in the country, this is usually a time consuming procedure.

Avoid taking international through routes between large cities, since this is far more expensive than a trip in two stages — a local bus to the border, and, after crossing the border, another local bus to your destination. Note that the borders are open during daylight hours only, with a break for the *siesta*. On weekends, the crossing points are open half-day at the most.

Hordes of money-changers congregate around the border check points. Before crossing the border, check the currency rates in the country you are about to enter, so that you won't be robbed blind by these money-changers. It is almost always better to change only as much money as you'll need to get to the nearest major city, since the rate offered by these border money-changers is low. On weekends, when banks are closed, you'll find yourself at the mercy of these money-changers, who take advantage of the situation and offer an even lower exchange rate.

At relevant points in the book, you will find guidelines regarding the various border crossing points and additional papers and documents you may need.

## Personal security

The social contrasts that are typical of Brazil (and most other Third World countries), have led to serious tension between the various strata of the population, and a plague of crime and violence. In the large cities, robbery and theft are routine events. Police efforts to fight crime have not been very successful. The scope and seriousness of the problem are brought home by the permanent presence of at least two armed guards at every bank branch, and by the fact that late at night cars do not stop at red lights for fear of robbers who might attack stationary cars.

Anyone visiting Brazil should adopt the basic precautionary measures that the locals are already used to: don't wear jewelry; carry your camera in your bag and guard the latter jealously; don't carry large sums of money with you; any extra money or documents should be deposited in the hotel safe. Do not rely on hotels and their employees. In many cases valuables that were innocently left in a hotel room have been stolen. If you are staying in the less expensive hotels that do not have safes, always take your money, documents, and important papers with you safely hidden under your clothes. It is a good idea to sew an inner pocket in your pants to hide valuables. Don't carry all your money in cash — at least some should be in travelers' checks (see "finance"). Never put your wallet in the back pocket of your trousers — a sore temptation to pickpockets — but always in a front pocket. In the large cities, stick to visiting the central and more pleasant areas, and avoid visiting the slums, or *favelas*. A visit to such places with any valuables whatsoever is tantamount to tempting fate. Likewise refrain from hitchhiking — especially if you are a woman by yourself.

In spite of all the above precautions, there is no reason to panic. Simply adhere to the guidelines above, and keep alert. In this way you will be able to complete an enjoyable and successful tour of Brazil without mishap or unpleasantness.

If you are nevertheless the victim of violence or crime, go to the nearest policeman or police station, and make sure to fill out the appropriate complaint form, in order to receive compensation from your insurance company.

## Shopping and souvenirs

Even confirmed tightwads will find it hard to resist the temptations of Brazil: the modern and luxurious shopping centers in the major cities offer the tourist a selection of high-quality goods at low prices, and the many markets to be found in every town are overflowing with attractive and interesting souvenirs and handicrafts (*artesania*) — each region with its own distinctive style.

Brazilian fashions excel in light, extremely colorful sportswear, which suit the tropical climate and the character of the people. Clothes are quite inexpensive, and you should certainly take the opportunity to renew your wardrobe with beautiful and comfortable summerwear. Leather goods, such as shoes and bags, are also inexpensive and of high quality.

Jewelry is a well-developed industry, thanks to the abundance of precious stones mined in Brazil. In the large cities there is a jewelry store on almost every street corner. These sell statuettes carved from various types of stone, all sorts of precious gems in various settings, and of course jewelry. All of these are extremely cheap in comparison to Western prices. Some of the largest jewelry chains in the world are Brazilian; the largest is *H. Stern*, which has a huge selection of jewelry of all kinds. Large stores too have a very wide selection — you will have no problem finding what you want — and they are less expensive than the jewelry stores.

As to souvenirs and handicrafts — each region in Brazil has its typical products: in the south, leather goods; in the southeast, particularly in Minas Gerais state, stone statuettes; in the northeast, beautiful, intricate lacework, wooden statuettes and wood carvings, and colorful hammocks. Pottery, typical Brazilian musical instruments, and shirts imprinted with local pictures or names can be found throughout Brazil. Indian souvenirs are found mainly in the regions where the Indians live, especially in the Amazon region, but they are ostentatious and reflect nothing of their lives. All types of handicrafts are sold throughout Brazil; for example, even in Rio you can find beautiful lacework. However, if you are intending to visit the north, wait until you get there — prices in the north are extremely low and you will be able to buy directly from the lacemaker herself.

In relevant sections you will find a detailed description of the various markets and villages and the typical handicrafts of each of them, as well as information about the large major shopping centers in the main towns. It would be hard to imagine that after visiting several of the places mentioned below you could leave Brazil empty-handed.

## Business hours

Brazilian banks are open Mon.-Fri., 10am-4:30pm, and closed on weekends. Stores are open Mon.-Fri., 9am-6:30pm, and on Saturdays till 1pm. During the holiday season, in December, most stores stay open until 10pm or even later. In the large modern shopping centers, the stores are open till late at night.

Outside the major cities, the situation is somewhat different. Hardly anyone skips the famous *siesta* (the traditional afternoon break customary throughout the Latin world), and most offices are closed in the afternoon for two or three hours.

## Measurements, electricity, and time

Brazil uses the metric system. Clothes are sized according to European measurements. Electricity is usually 110V, but always check before using an electrical appliance, since many areas have gone over to 220V. Brazil's official time is set by the time in Brasília, GMT-3, but due to the vast size of the country, in the west the clock is set an hour later.

## Suggested itinerary for Brazil

Each chapter of the guide is based on a geographical route, and each new chapter continues from where the previous chapter ended. Thus there is a geographic continuity between the two main routes — the southern route and the northern route. Of course, you can compile your own itinerary according to personal preferences within different regions, or you can combine a selection of sites from different chapters.

Southern route — Rio de Janeiro, São Paulo, Southern Brazil, Foz do Iguacu.

Northern route — Minas Gerais, north to Salvador, north-eastern Brazil, Amazon Basin and south to the Midwest. This tour ends in the new capital of Brasília.

For those who do not wish to explore the depths of the Amazon Jungle (which is particularly difficult to do overland), we suggest an alternative route from Rio de Janeiro westwards: Minas Gerais, Brasília, Pantanal.

We will become acquainted with north-eastern Brazil through a tour of the coast from southern Salvador northwards to São Luis.

The tour of the Amazon Basin goes from Belem to Manaus, and there you can choose one of three possible directions to take: north to Boa Vista and on to Venezuela; west to Benjamin Constant, Leticia and on to Colombia or Peru; south to Porto Velho. It's a short way from Porto Velho to Bolivia or you can go towards the Midwest, to Cuiaba. We have outlined all these possibilities, but the main route along which we will continue our tour is that which goes to Porto Velho and to the Midwest.

# BRAZIL

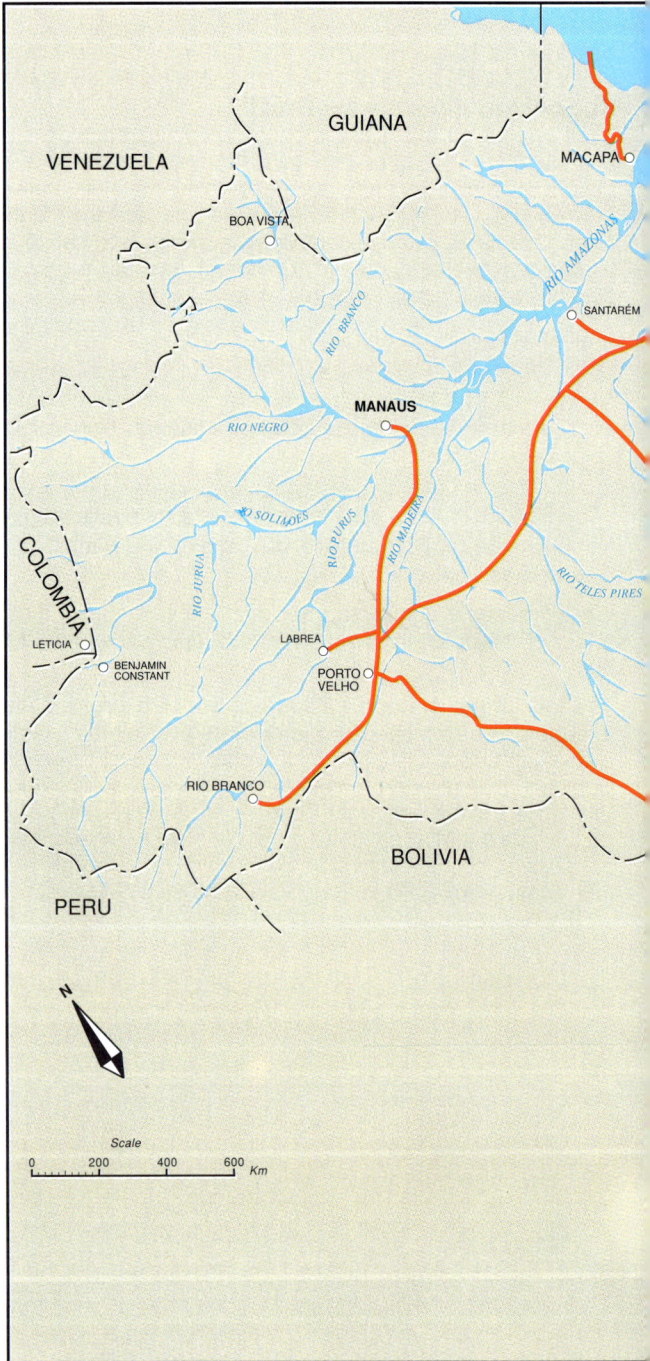

VENEZUELA

GUIANA

MACAPA

BOA VISTA

RIO AMAZONAS

SANTARÉM

RIO BRANCO

MANAUS

RIO NEGRO

COLOMBIA

RIO SOLIMÕES

RIO PURUS

RIO JURUA

RIO MADEIRA

RIO TELES PIRES

LETICIA

BENJAMIN
CONSTANT

LABREA

PORTO
VELHO

RIO BRANCO

BOLIVIA

PERU

N

Scale
0      200      400      600  Km

A map of eastern and southern Brazil showing cities and road/river networks.

BELÉM

FORTALEZA
ARACATI
NATAL
JOÃO PESSOA
OLINDA
SÃO LUÍS
CAMPINA GRANDE
RECIFE
TERESINA
CRATEUS
JUAZEIRO DO NORTE
CARUARU
MACEIO
ARACAJU
RIO TOCANTINS
RIO PARAÍBA
RIO SÃO FRANCISCO
JUAZEIRO
FEIRA DE SANTANA
SALVADOR
ILHEUS
ITAPETINGA
GUANAMBI
PORTO SEGURO
RIO DAS MORTES
RIO ARAGUAIA
BRASÍLIA
GOVERNADOR VALADARES
VITORIA
GOIANIA
BELO HORIZONTE
OURO PRETO
ARAGUARI
CAMPOS
UBERABA
JUIZ DE FORA
PETROPOLIS
RIBEIRAO PRETO
BARRA MANSA
NITEROI
ARACATUBA
ARAQUARA
SÃO CARLOS
TABUATE
RIO DE JANEIRO
CAMPO GRANDE
BAURU
LIMEIRA
PANTANAL
TRES LAGOAS
MARILIA
SOROCABA
SÃO PAULO
SANTOS
SÃO VICENTE
PRESIDENTE PRUDENTE
LONDRINA
CURITIBA
PONTA GROSSA
PARANAGUÁ
JOINVILLE
ITAJAI
ARAGUAY
FOZ DO IGUAÇU
PATO BRANCO
FLORIANOPOLIS
TUBARAO
CRICIUMA
PASSO FUNDO
ARAGUAIA
SANTO ANGELO
CAXIAS DO SUL
S. LEOPOLDO
SANTA MARIA
PORTO ALEGRE
SÃO BORJA
CACHOEIRA
LAGOA DOS PATOS
ALEGRETE
DOM PEDRITO
PELOTAS
URUGUAIANA
BAJE
RIO GRANDE
SANTANA DO LIVRAMENTO
ARGENTINA
URUGUAY

51

# $B$ RAZIL

## Rio de Janeiro

Many people consider Rio to be one of the most beautiful cities on earth. Its southern neighborhoods cluster between steep, verdant cliffs hundreds of meters high and broad sandy beaches. As if nature had not provided enough delights, the city's residents have added all kinds of attractions of their own. During the day shopping centers are bustling, and the wonderful beaches are packed, and at night the restaurants, clubs and discotheques overflow. The locals are nicknamed "*Carioca*", and they enjoy a reputation for being both amiable and good-looking, with their tanned complexions and bright and colorful dress.

The French were the first to settle here in 1555. During the subsequent 150 years or so, the city experienced many upheavals and reversals as it passed from French to Portuguese rule. Rio came under Portuguese control in the early 18th century, and by the middle of that century it had become the seat of the Portuguese Governor. It was declared capital of the Republic of Brazil in 1834, and retained this title until the establishment of Brasília in 1960. Today the city has a population of about six million, and is constantly developing and growing. The presence of rich, elegant and exclusive neighborhoods alongside impoverished *favelas* (shantytowns) has given rise to great social tensions and Rio has a high rate of crime and violence.

Rio's summers are uncomfortably hot and humid, with temperatures up to 40°C (104°F) and frequent showers. Winter, from May to October, is more temperate, with warm weather and usually clear skies. Average maximum temperature in these months is 25°C (75°F).

Area code: 021

### How to get there
**By air:** Rio has two busy airports. The first is the **Aeroporto Internacional do Galeão** at Ilha do Governador, about half an hour drive out of town. The terminal has three sections: A for domestic flights, and B and C for international

*Sunset in Rio de Janeiro*

flights. It is an excellent, modern airport with heavy traffic every day from all over the world. *Varig* fly daily to New York, Los Angeles and Miami. Many European airlines also connect Rio to all major European cities, and there are weekly *Varig* and *SAA* flights to South Africa. There are also daily flights to all South American capitals. At the airport there are many radio-taxis that can convey you quickly and comfortably to any destination in town for fixed fares. Comfortable buses, with much lower fares, leave every few minutes for different parts of Rio.

The other airport is **Santos Dumont**, located downtown. This small airfield, serving only the shuttle service between Rio and São Paulo, is connected to the rest of Rio by many taxis, and regular and special buses.

**By land:** The bus terminal, *Rodoviaria Novo Rio* in the São Cristovão neighborhood, is served by buses from all over Brazil and from Buenos Aires (Argentina), Montevideo (Uruguay), Asuncion (Paraguay), and Santiago (Chile). It's always busy and, despite its size, very crowded. There are many taxis in the vicinity, and many city bus lines start here too.

## Tourist services

Two municipal tourist bureaus provide information for visitors to Rio. One is *Embratur*, the Brazilian Tourist Bureau, at Rua Mariz Barros 13, close to Praça de Bandeira in northern Rio (tel. 273-2212, open Mon.-Fri. 9am-6pm). The other bureau is *Riotur*, the Rio de Janeiro Tourist Bureau, at Rua Assemblia 10 (tel. 297-7117). *Riotur* has another office downtown, at Rua São José 90 (tel. 232-4320), and provides 24-hour telephone service in English, French, and Spanish (tel. 580-8000). There are also information booths at various locations around the city such as the Sugarloaf cablecar, the Novo Rio bus terminal, and the International Airport.

*Touring Club do Brasil* is on Avenida General Serviano in Botafogo. Here you can find up-to-date information about Brazil in general and Rio in particular.

Most airline offices in Rio are concentrated around Avenida Rio Branco downtown. *Varig*, Brazil's national airline, has many offices throughout the city.

There are many car rental companies in Rio so you should have no problem finding a suitable car. The largest and most reliable international companies are *Avis* and *Hertz*, and the best Brazilian companies are *Localiza* and *Nobre*. All have branch offices at the International Airport. In town, their offices are on Avenida Princesa Isabel in Copacabana. The rates are much higher than in the United States or Europe, and bear in mind that gas stations are closed on weekends.

## Where to stay
Rio has an abundance of hotels of all kinds, from the most superb and expensive to the very low-priced for young travelers. Downtown hotels look attractive, mainly for youngsters wishing to economize, but the area by night is deserted and lonely, and quite unpleasant, and furthermore, far from the night-spots in the south of town. There are some very inexpensive hotels with basic facilities in the Catete Quarter, which is a cut above downtown.

### Luxury Hotels
*Caesar Park*: Av. Vieira Souto 460, Ipanema; tel. 287-3122, fax 247-7975. Paraliel to the Ipanema beach, one of the best equiped.

*Rio Palace*: Av. Atlantica 4240, Copacabana; tel. 521-3232, fax 227-1454. At the southern end of Copacabana, is considered one of the best in town, with a great view over Copacabana and Ipanema, and all the facilities hotels of this kind can offer.

*Sheraton Rio*: Av. Niemeyer 121; tel. 274-1122, fax 239-5643, located in a very pleasant location, on the slopes between Leblon and São Conrado. Although far from the ''in'' places, all the possibilities are inside the complex: a sports centre, a private beach, swimming pool, tennis courts, discotheque, and even a small zoo.

*Inter-Continental*: Av. Pref. Mendes de Morais 222, São Conrado; tel. 322-2200, fax 322-500. First class, with three swimming pools, two bars, a good restaurant, discotheque, sports club and tennis courts.

*Le Meridien*: Av. Atlantica 1020, Copacabaca; tel. 275-9922, fax 541-6447. It offers superb facilities, and one of the best French restaurants in town.

### Expensive
*Rio Othon Palace*: Av. Atlantica 3264; tel. 521-5522, fax 521-6697. A tall building in the middle of Copacabana. Good services, beautiful views from its top where there is a small swimming pool and a bar.

*Copacabana Palace*: Av. Atlantica 1702; tel. 255-7070, fax 235-7330.

*Nacional Rio*: Av. Niemeyer 769, São Conrado; tel. 322-1000, fax 322-058. One of the jewels of the HORSA chain, is outstanding, and holds one of the largest convention centres in Brazil.

*Gloria*: Rua do Russel 632, Gloria; tel. 205-7272, fax 245-1660.

It proves very convenient for those looking for the downtown area, it maintains a high standard.

*Sol Ipanema*: Av. Vieira Souto 320, Ipanema; tel. 267-0095, fax 247-1685. Close to the beach and to the better places of Ipanema.

*Marina Rio*: Av. Delfim Moreira 696, Leblon; tel. 239-8844. Offer attractive views, close to the beach and to many night spots.

*Marina Palace*: Av. Delfim Moreira 630, Leblon; tel. 205-7272, fax 245-1660. Under the same management as the former hotel, but a better and more expensive one.

## Moderate

*Debret*: Av. Atlantica 3564; tel. 521-3332, fax 521-0899. It overlooks the beach; superb view. Fine service, rooms, and location; recommended.

*Novo Mundo*: Praia do Flamengo 20; tel. 205-3355, fax 265-2369. In the Gloria quarter, it is quite inexpensive, providing basic but good facilities. Far from the city's better beaches and night spots.

*Copacabana Sol*: Rua Santa Clara 141, Copacabana; tel. 257-1840. Relatively low prices, not far from the beach.

*Arpoador Inn*: Rua Francisco Otaviano 177, Arpoador (between Copacabana and Ipanema); tel. 247-6090.

*Carlton*: Rua João Lira 68, Leblon; tel. 259-1932. Noteworthy for its pleasant, tranquil atmosphere, close to the beach.

*Astoria*: Av. Republica do Peru 345, Copacabana; tel. 257-8080. Moderately priced, but the facilities offered do not justify the price.

## Inexpensive

*Ipanema Inn*: Rua Maria Quiteria 27, Ipanema; tel. 287-6092. Good location.

*Martinique*: Rua Sá Ferreira 30, Copacabana; tel. 521-4552. Good location near the Rio Palace, close to both Copacabana and Ipanema.

*Toledo*: Rua Domingos Ferreira 71, Copacabana; tel. 257-1990. Close to the beach, comfortable rooms.

*Florida*: Rua Ferreira Viana 69, Flamengo; tel. 245-8160.

*San Marco*: Rua Visconde de Piraja 524, Ipanema; tel. 239-5032. A cheap hotel near the beach, with a young staff; a comfortable place to stay.

Many inexpensive hotels with very basic facilities can be found in the Catete Quarter, between Gloria and Flamengo. The place for the *muchileros* to look for a room (be sure to see your room before checking in).

*The marvelous view from the Corcovado*

## Where to eat

Rio has many good restaurants and, as an international metropolis, provides excellent examples of European, Easter and Latin American cuisine. The range of prices is wide, and everyone can find a place according to his budget. Most of the fancy restaurants are in Ipanema and Leblon, or in the five-star hotels, while in Catete, Botafogo and downtown, you can find the cheap *churrascarias* and **lanchonetes**. Fast-food lovers can rely on one of the many branches of McDonald's and other chains.

*Du Nil*: Rua da Alfandega 375, Centro; tel. 224-7325. Open for lunch, except Sundays and holidays. Arabian food.
*Hansi*: Rua Prof. Lohman 132; tel. 399-0279. Open for dinner, closed on Mondays. Central European food. Alto do Joá, not far from Barra da Tijuca.
*Mr. Zee*: Av. Gen. San Martin 1219, Leblon; tel. 294-6240. Open for dinner, good Chinese food.
*Claude Troisgros*: Rua Custodio Serrao 62, Jardim Botanico; tel. 226-4542. Dinner in a French, luxury style. One of the best, and expensive, restaurants in town.
*Enotria*: Rua C. Ramos 115, Copacabana; tel. 237-6705. Superb Italian cuisine, for dinner only, closed Sunday.

**By cable-car to the Sugarloaf**

*Quadrifoglio*: Rua Maria Angelica 43, Jardim Botanico; tel. 226-1799. Another excellent Italian restaurant. Only for those who do not care about calories.

*Komatsu*: Av. Rio Branco 156, Centro; tel. 240-8793. Lunch during the week, Japanese food.

*Associação Macrobiotica*: Rua Emb. Oliveira 7, Centro; tel. 220-7585. During the week, a modest and inexpensive macrobiotic lunch.

*Natural*: Rua Br. da Torre 171, Ipanema; tel. 267-7799. Naturalist. There is another branch in Botafogo — Rua 19 de Fevreiro 118; tel. 226-9898. The former is open for lunch and dinner, the latter — for lunch only.

*Clube Gourmet*: Rua Polidoro 186, Botafogo; tel. 295-3494. Highly recommended, expensive.

*Casa de Suiça*: Rua Candido Mendes 157, Gloria; tel. 252-5182. Swiss food.

*Antiquarius*: Rua Espinola 19, Leblon; tel. 294-1049. Portuguese cusine. Highly recommended.

*Buffalo Grill*: Rua Rita Ludolf 47, Leblon; tel. 274-4848. One of the best *churrascarias* in Rio.

*Marius*: Av. Atlântica 290-B, Leme; tel. 542-2393. Another good *churrascaria*, on the Copacabana see-front. Rodízio.

Many good seafood restaurants can be found in the outskirts of town, close to the beach; among them:

*Candido's*: Rua Barros de Alarcao 352; tel. 395-1630, in Pedra de Guaratiba.

*Tia Palmira*, cam. do Souza 18; tel. 410-1169; in Barra de Guaratiba. Inexpensive.

*Café do Teatro*: Av. Rio Branco, Centro, at the Teatro municipal; tel. 262-4164. Special classic decoration, good food. Open for lunch, closed weekends.

*La Tour*: Rua Santa Luiza 651, Centro; tel. 240-5493. A revolving restaurant on the 34th floor of a high-rise building. Spectacular views; the food, however, is nothing special.

*Le Saint Honoré*: Av. Atlântica 1020, Leme; tel. 275-9922. At the 37th floor of the Merdien. Excellent French menu, good service, beautiful panorama. Expensive.

*Shirley*: Rua Gustavo Sampaio 610, Leme; tel. 275-1398. Although its setting doesn't seem very promising, the Spanish menu seafood is very good, service is friendly and prices are reasonable.

## Getting around town

**Taxis** are always available in Rio, and fares are very low. Regular taxis have two tariffs: one for regular trips, and another for service after midnight, on Sundays, or to the airport. Make sure the meter does not display Tariff 2 when making a regular trip. The sum shown on the meter is not the price you pay; it has to be multiplied according to the table of fares which the driver has. Be sure to check the price!

Another type of taxi is the radio-taxi — a large, air-conditioned vehicle ordered by telephone. The largest radio-taxi companies are *Coopertramo* (tel. 260-2022), *Cootramo* (tel. 270-1442), and *Transcoopass* (tel. 270-4888).

**Buses** are fast, regular, and frequent, and they reach every corner of the city. Each bus is numbered and carries route details. Drivers are polite and always willing to give information. They usually stop for pedestrians who hail them down in between stops. Many routes start from the inter-city bus terminal.

Rio also has a **subway** (metro) which is clean and pleasant. There are only two lines, linking Botafogo with downtown and northern Rio. The metro runs 6am-11pm every day except Sunday, and is quick, comfortable and safe (not late at night).

## What to see

Before setting off to explore Rio's beaches and neighborhoods, visit two outstandingly beautiful observation points — perhaps the most famous tourist spots in Rio and indeed in all Brazil:

the Corcovado and Sugarloaf Mountain. Each provides a spectacular view of the city. From these points it is clear why Rio is considered the world's most beautiful city.

## Corcovado

This is certainly the place that springs to mind when Rio de Janeiro is mentioned. Corcovado is the famous mount whose summit, 709 m above sea level, bears a giant statue of Jesus that is clearly visible from almost any point in the city. (Many people mistakenly apply the name Corcovado to the statue, instead of the hill.) The statue is 30 m tall and is made of 1450 tons of concrete and granite, with an observation deck at its base. At night the statue is spotlit and stands out dramatically against the black sky. No visit to Rio would be complete without a visit to Corcovado.

The left hand of the statue points in the direction of the northern city, the commercial and business area. Notice in the distance the International Airport, the immense Rio-Niteroi bridge, the Maracana Stadium, the Santos Dumont Airport, and the wide avenues and skyscrapers of downtown. Opposite stands proud Sugarloaf Mountain. Between Sugarloaf and downtown is the Flamengo neighborhood, and between Sugarloaf and Corcovado is Botafogo. Copacabana is on the right.

The statue's right hand points in the direction of Ipanema and Leblon, and, at the foot of Corcovado, one can see the Botanical Gardens, the Jockey Club, and the lake — Lagoa Rodrigo de Freitas.

There are two ways of getting to Corcovado: by road or by train. The train station is at Rua Cosme Velho 513, and there are trains every half-hour between 8am and 10pm. They cover the 3.5 km distance in about 20 minutes, traveling through a beautiful landscape of thick, luxuriant foliage. The lower station is reached by Bus 583 from Copacabana. The road also winds up the mountain through wonderful scenery. There is a parking lot close to the summit and nearby there are cafes and souvenir shops.

The best time to visit Corcovado is toward evening, when the sun is setting behind you and the fantastic view is seen against the backdrop of spreading darkness and city lights.

## Pão de Açúcar — Sugarloaf Mountain

After the spectacular view from the Corcovado, no one will want to miss a visit to Sugarloaf Mountain, which gives a different perspective of the city. Sugarloaf is an immense granite slab at the entrance of the Guanabara Bay. Its walls rise steeply to a

## *RIO DE JANEIRO — CENTRO*

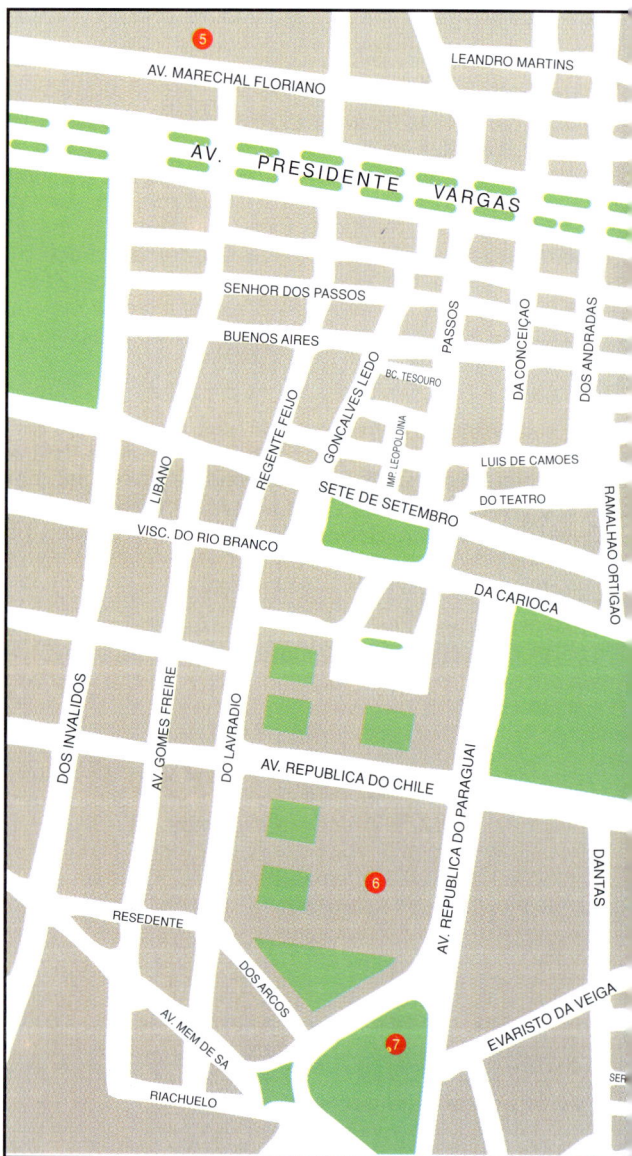

**Index**

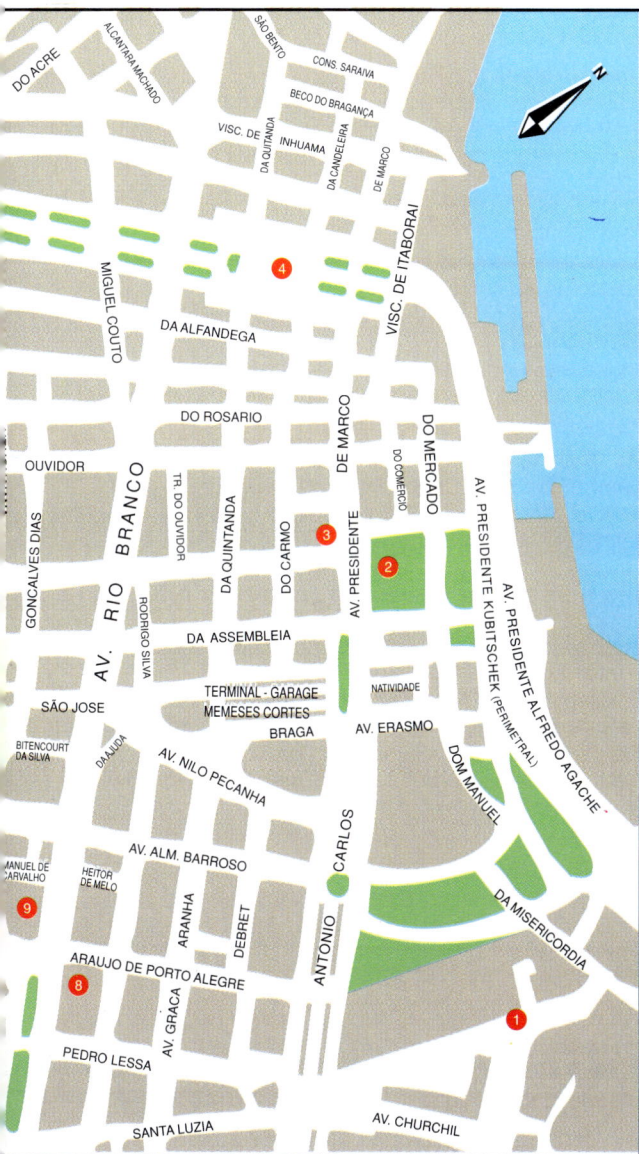

6. Nova Catedral
   Metropolitana
7. Agueduto da Carioca

8. Museu Nacional
   de Belas Artes
9. Teatro Municipal

height of 396 m above sea level, from which the whole city can be observed. At twilight, crowds of amateur and professional photographers come here to catch the fabulous sunsets.

A cablecar starts out from Praça General Tiburcio at the Vermelho beach, with departures every thirty minutes. Halfway up is Morro da Urca, where there is an entertainment center with a discotheque and samba performances (see "Nightlife").

Do not choose a cloudy day for either of these observation points, in which case both are hidden in clouds.

Having seen Rio and its beauty from the heights, let us study it from close up.

### The Northern City
This is a dreary, unpleasant concentration of industrial and poor neighborhoods, but there are two sites here that should not be missed: Quinta Boa Vista and Estadio Maracana.

**Quinta Boa Vista** (Boa Vista Palace) houses the **Museu Nacional**, Rio's most important and interesting museum. The impressive palace was built in 1803 by a wealthy Portuguese gentleman who presented it as a gift to his King in 1808. It was a residence of the Brazilian monarchs until the country became a republic in 1889. A few years later, in 1892, it was turned into a National Museum. On display is a wealth of exhibits: archaeology, botany, zoology, ethnology, and more. Most interesting of all are the South American archaeology halls, especially that devoted to Brazil, and the exhibits of Indian ethnology and Brazilian folklore. In the entrance hall stands the largest meteorite ever found in the southern hemisphere, discovered in Bahia in 1888. (Open Tues.-Sun., 10am-4:45pm.) The Boa Vista Palace is in the São Cristovão neighborhood. Take Bus 472 or 474 from Copacabana, or 262 from downtown.

Close to the National Museum is the **Zoo**, and across from its entrance is an interesting **Zoological Museum** with a selection of wildlife from the different regions of Brazil, particularly from the Amazon and the Pantanal (open Tues.-Sun. 9am-4:30pm; tel. 254-2024.)

Not far from the National Museum, in Campo de São Cristovão, the **Feira do Nordeste** (market of northeastern Brazil) takes place every Sunday. Here the people of northern Brazil sell their various wares at low prices. It's hot and dirty, but fascinating.

Another interesting place in this area is the **Estadio Maracanã** (Maracanã Stadium), or Mario Filho Stadium. Built for the 1950 World Cup Finals in Rio, it is the world's biggest stadium with seating for 200,000. It is also very well planned, so that even the last rows are not far from the playing field. In the premises you can visit a small museum of the Sports, along with the stadium itself (open to visitors Mon.-Fri., 9am-4pm; tel. 264-9962.) Nearby is another stadium, the **Maracanazinho**, or "Little Maracana", which can seat 20,000 spectators. It accommodates basketball and volleyball courts, and also entertainment events.

## Centro
This is Rio's large, important business and commercial hub. During the day it bustles with workers and business people, but it empties out after working hours. Once that happens, it is best not to wander about its dark and lonely streets.

The first landmark in the Centro is to the right of the freeway leading in from the south. On the northern edge of Flamengo Park is a monument to the fallen of World War II (Brazil fought alongside the Allies in the Italian campaign, in which 467 soldiers lost their lives). Close to the memorial is a small museum which commemorates the Brazilian soldiers' contribution to the war effort.

A little past the monument is the **Museu de Arte Moderna** — MAM (open Tues.-Sun., noon-4pm; tel. 210-2188). This was one of the most important museums in Brazil until 1978, when a disastrous fire destroyed almost all of its very fine collection. The museum has not succeeded in rehabilitating itself, and its value as an artistic institution has declined.

Not far from the Museu de Arte Moderna, on Praça Marechal Ancora, is the **Museu Historico Nacional**. The building is one of the oldest in Rio, erected in the early 17th century as the São Diego Fortress. The museum was established in 1922, as part of the celebrations for 100 years of Brazilian independence. Brazil's most important historical museum, it presents the country's history since its discovery (open Tues.-Fri., 10am-5:30pm, weekends 2:30-5:30pm, closed Mon.; tel. 220-2628).

Not far from the Museum is **Praça Quince de Novembro**, a site where a number of historical events took place. Here King Dom João VI of Portugal stepped ashore in 1808 after Portugal fell to Napoleon. From here, too, his grandson, Dom Pedro II of Brazil, sailed back to Europe on November 15, 1891, when Brazil changed from an empire to a republic. Today, a ferry sails from the dock at the end of the square to Niteroi and Paqueta. On the southern edge of the square is the Commissioners' Palace, built in 1743 in colonial style. This was the first residence of the King of Portugal in Brazil. After it was renovated a few years ago, the building became the headquarters of the postal and telegraph services. The church on the west side of the square is the old **Catedral Metropolitana** (built in 1671), where Pedro I was crowned in December, 1822. At the northern end of the square is the **Arco de Teles**. The arch was built in the 18th century. It is all that remains of a Senate building that was destroyed by fire. Pass through and come out on a little side street, **Travessa do Comercio**, where time seems to stand still. Even today, it is a quiet, tranquil pedestrian mall, quite different from the rest of the area.

**Avenida Presidente Vargas**, once the widest boulevard in South America, still hums with people and commercial activities. Standing here, we feel the pulse of this large and lively metropolis. On the central island stands the **Igreja de Candelaria**, one of the city's most famous churches. On the parallel street, at Avenida Marechal Floriano 196, is the **Museu Diplomatico (Itamarati)** — a splendid palace built by Baron Itamarati in 1852. When the Republic came into being, it purchased the palace and turned it into a presidential residence. In 1897 another mansion was set aside for the President, and the Itamarati became the home of the Foreign Ministry until 1970, when all Government ministries moved to the new national capital of Brasília. Since then, the building has housed a museum displaying Brazil's past as well as its own (temporarily closed; tel. 291-4411).

Continue to the **Nova Catedral Metropolitana** at the corner of Paraguai and Chile Avenues. The huge church was built between 1964 and 1976 at the site of Mount São Antonio. By a tremendous feat of engineering, the hill was moved to Flamengo, to an area which is now Flamengo Park. Close to the church is the **Aqueduto da Carioca**, a structure 64 m high, built in the mid-18th century. Originally used to carry water from the Rio Cosme Velho to downtown Rio, it was converted in 1896 into a road linking the Centro with the Santa Terese neighborhood.

Finally, we explore **Avenida Rio Branco**, one of the important thoroughfares in town. Most of the airline offices, as well as Rio's black market, are found here. In 1904, hundreds of houses were destroyed in order to built the broad, busy boulevard, and until a few years ago, when a special route was built for the purpose, the Samba parade thundered down this artery, too. At Rio Branco 199 is the **Museu Nacional de Belas Artes** (Fine Arts Museum). Founded in 1837, it houses one of the best and most important collections of Brazilian art (open Tues.-Fri. noon-6pm, weekends and holidays 3-6pm.; tel. 240-0068).

Near the museum stands the magnificent **Teatro Municipal**, built in 1905 on the model of the Paris Opera, it is the venue of symphony concerts, ballet and opera.

*A view from the Sugarloaf*

**Flamengo and Botafogo**

Until the 1940s, Flamengo and Botafogo (the southern extension of Flamengo) were considered the most prestigious neighborhoods of Rio. Today, other parts, like Ipanema and Leblon has eclipsed them, and they have become rather drab residential districts. Flamengo regained some of its prestige, through the artificial expansion of the Flamengo beach. Along the wide beach is a pleasant green park which is used by *Cariocas* for sports. The park extends from the Santos Dumont airport in the north to Botafogo in the south. In 1960, over a million cubic meters of earth were moved here from Mount São Antonio to create this stretch of land. Do not walk around here at night, as it is dark and dangerous.

North of the park are the **Modern Art Museum** and the **World War II Memorial** (see "Centro").

The beaches of Flamengo and Botafogo are among the least attractive in Rio. The bay water is polluted, and most of the people who use the facility are from the city's poor northern neighborhoods, which are closer to here. All the area can offer is a few museums, the most interesting of which is the **Museu da Republica**, at Rua do Catete 179 in Flamengo. It is housed in the Palacio do Catete, built in 1866 in neoclassical style for use as a residence by the Brazilian aristocracy. It was purchased in 1896 by the Republic for the President. The museum exhibits the history of Brazil from the founding of the Republic to 1960, when the Presidential residence moved to the new capital, Brasília (open Tues.-Sun. noon-5pm; tel. 225-4302).

The **Museu do Indio** is at Rua das Palmeiras 55 in Botafogo. April 19 is Indians Day in Brazil, and the museum opened on that date in 1953. It displays artifacts of Indian tribes from Brazil's various areas, including the culture and folklore that developed in each region. It's an interesting museum, but the explanations are only given in Portuguese (open Tues.-Fri. 10am-6pm, Sat. and Sun. 1-5pm; tel. 286-8799).

## Zona Sul

*Zona Sul*, the south of Rio, is a prestigious residential area interspersed with many commercial centers. In the 1940s and 1950s, **Copacabana** was the most exclusive area of the city, but today even the charms of the famous 4 km Copacabana Beach have palled in the eyes of the *Carioca*, who now prefer new seashore haunts.

The northern neighborhood of this part of town, from Morro do Leme to Avenida Princesa Isabel, is called Leme. Along Avenida Atlantica, parallel to the beach, are many classy hotels, homes and places of entertainment in high-rises which form a kind of wall against the sea. This lovely beach is not natural; it was transformed in part by human hand into the attractive, broad stretch of sand we see today.

**Ipanema** and **Leblon** are presently the most exclusive residential areas of the city, with magnificent apartment houses, luxurious shops, and boutiques lining the main boulevard. Superb restaurants and bars are located on the side streets.

On Sundays, the **Hippie Fair** is held at Praça General Osorio in Ipanema. This is a delightful market where *objets d'art*, musical instruments, leather goods, and much more are on sale. Prices are high, and the bargaining is tough. Some of these typical offerings are available elsewhere in Brazil at much lower prices. Nevertheless, the market is worth a visit, if only to enjoy the pleasant atmosphere and inspect the handicrafts.

Avenida Visconde de Piraja is the main shopping center of Ipanema. Here, at the corner of Garcia d'Avila, is the H. Stern building, one of the world's largest headquarters of the *H. Stern* jewelry chain. Brazil's ample natural resources include gems of many kinds, and the Stern company controls over 60 percent of this trade. It is a fascinating place to visit. Watch the stones being polished, and inspect the company's best wares in its elegant showroom.

The beaches of Ipanema and Leblon are actually one stretch of very fine beach about 2 km long and only slightly narrower than the Copacabana beach. This is where Rio's upper classes and, of course, its beauties come to bathe. The boulevard along the beach is lined with homes and a few prestigious hotels. Unlike Copacabana, most hotels and all the nightspots here are on the side streets.

The Jardim de Ala canal separates Ipanema from Leblon and connects the sea with Lagoa Rodrigo de Freitas, called **Lagoa** (Lake) for short. The lake, covers 4500 sq/m, is situated at the foot of soaring cliffs covered with tropical foliage. West of Lagoa is the **Joquei Clube Brasileiro**, the Jockey Club, which has a particularly fine race-track (see "Sports"). Beyond it is the **Jardim Botânico**, with a fantastic collection of plants and trees from all over the world. One can spend hours strolling through the gardens and enjoying their delights (open Tues.-Sun., 8am-5pm; closed during Carnival).

**São Conrado:** Leblon is separated from São Conrado on the west by a mountainous ridge. This ridge is crossed by two roads; one along the coast which is double decker and beautiful (worth the trip for itself), and the other heading through a tunnel. The São Conrado quarter is another wealthy and prestigious residential area, with three excellent hotels. The beach here is known as Praia do Pepino — Cucumber Beach. Its far (western) end is the landing place of the hang-glider, who launch from the tremendous cliffs high above. It is considered to be one of the best hang-gliding sites in the world.

### Floresta da Tijuca

This forest is the largest park in Rio, covering more than 120 sq/km in the Corcovado area and the hills to its west. It is an area of luxuriant jungle foliage, steep granite cliffs, rivers, and waterfalls. The hills range in height from 100 to 1020 m above sea level, giving the park a cooler and more pleasant climate than that of the city itself.

There are some wonderful observation points in the park, the best of which is Alto da Boa Vista. There are many ways to reach this point; the nicest is the ascent from the Botanical Gardens. This route passes another two attractions: **Vista Chinesa**, and **Mesa do Imperador**. They are so called because of unsuccessful attempts by Chinese to grow tea here in the days of Dom Pedro II. Walk along the park's paths and enjoy

# RIO DE JANEIRO — ZONA SUL

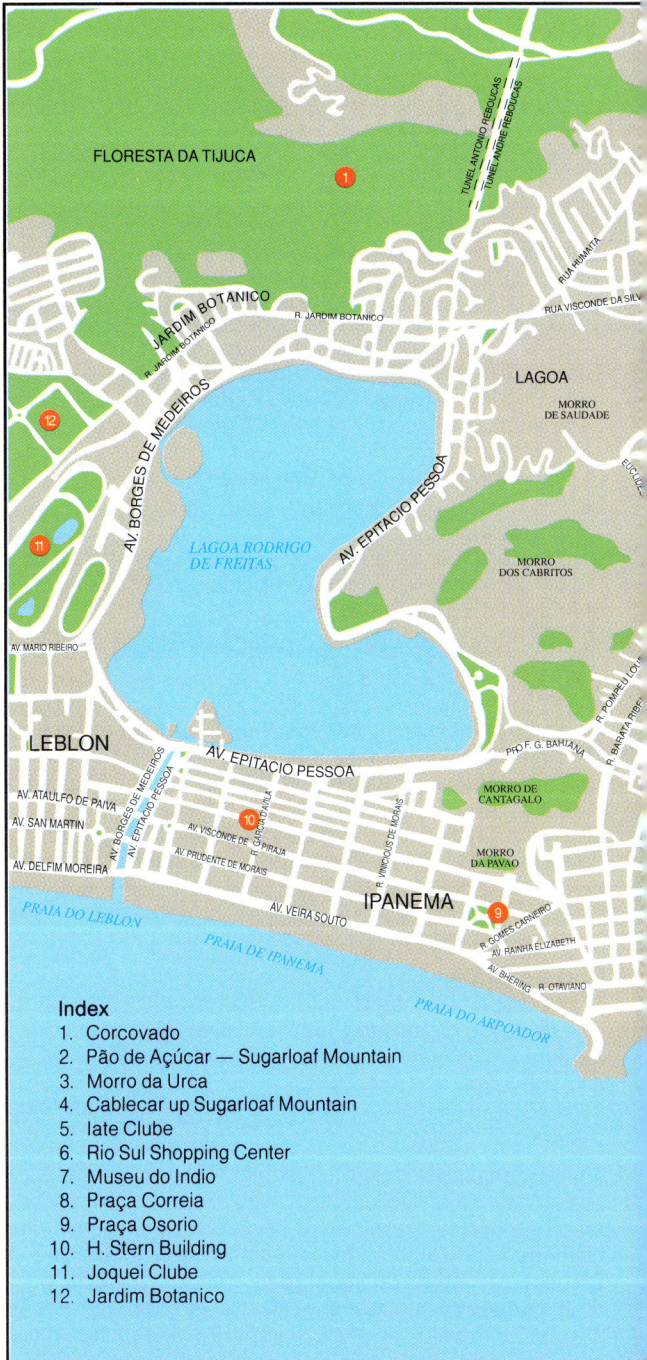

FLORESTA DA TIJUCA

TUNEL ANTONIO REBOUCAS
TUNEL ANDRE REBOUCAS

RUA HUMATA

JARDIM BOTANICO
R. JARDIM BOTANICO
R. JARDIM BOTANICO

RUA VISCONDE DA SILV

LAGOA

MORRO
DE SAUDADE

AV. BORGES DE MEDEIROS

AV. EPITACIO PESSOA

EUCLIDE

*LAGOA RODRIGO
DE FREITAS*

MORRO
DOS CABRITOS

R. POMPEU LO

R. BARATA RIBE

AV. MARIO RIBEIRO

LEBLON

AV. EPITACIO PESSOA

PPO F. G. BAHIANA

AV. ATAULFO DE PAIVA

AV. BORGES DE MEDEIROS

AV. EPITACIO PESSOA

R. GARCIA DHLA

AV. VISCONDE DE

MORRO DE
CANTAGALO

AV. SAN MARTIN

AV. PRUDENTE DE MORAIS

R. VINICIUS DE MORAIS

MORRO
DA PAVAO

AV. DELFIM MOREIRA

IPANEMA

AV. VEIRA SOUTO

R. GOMES CARNEIRO

AV. RAINHA ELIZABETH

*PRAIA DO LEBLON*

*PRAIA DE IPANEMA*

AV. BHERING  R. OTAVIANO

*PRAIA DO ARPOADOR*

## Index

# FLAMENGO

PALMEIRAS

**7**

RUA VOLUNTÁRIOS DA PÁTRIA

AVENIDA DAS NAÇÕES UNIDAS

*BOTAFOGO BAY*

## BOTAFOGO

AV. PASTEUR

**5**

AVENIDA PORTUGAL

R. MAL. CANTUÁRIA

**2**

MORRO
DO URCA

**3**

AV. VENCESLAU BRÁS

**6**

**4**

MORRO DA
BABILÔNIA

MORRO
DE SÃO
JOÃO

PRINCESA ISABEL

LADEIRA DO LEME

MORRO DO
URUBU

## LEME

MORRO
DO
LEME

R. TONELEIRO

RUA BARATA RIBEIRO

RUA GUSTAVO SAMPAIO

AVENIDA NOSSA SENHORA DE COPACABANA

**AVENIDA ATLÂNTICA**

*PRAIA DO LEME*

DO MIGUEZ

**8**

## COPACABANA

ES SALDANHA

AVENIDA ATLÂNTICA

*PRAIA DE COPACABANA*

*ATLANTIC OCEAN*

N

the tranquil atmosphere. The park is open 7am-7pm. There are two restaurants within the park. Don't stay after dark.

## Nightlife

In planning your daily schedule, bear in mind that your day does not end at sunset. Maybe the contrary is true: for many *cariocas* the sunset is when their day begins. Rio offers a varied and rich assortment of activities, from all kinds of light amusement to opera and chamber music.

**Theater, Concerts, Opera:** Despite the prevailing impression that Rio's night life is nothing but night-clubbing and discos, the city has no shortage of more classical forms of entertainment. Ballet fans will find a very good dance company that performs at the luxurious Teatro Municipal downtown. This venue is also used by the city opera, an excellent company which hosts international guest singers, from time to time. Symphony concerts take place at the Teatro, while chamber concerts and recitals are held in the smaller Sala Cecilia on Largo da Lapa, also in the *Centro*. Local theater, though of great variety, is not a good idea for those who do not understand Portuguese.

**Cinema:** Films are shown in their original languages with Portuguese subtitles, and popular European and American movies reach Rio shortly after their original release. Movie theaters proliferate in all parts of Rio, and most are very satisfactory. Tickets cannot be bought in advance, and on weekends there are long lines at box offices.

**Samba:** This is the kind of entertainment for which most tourists really come to Rio. The excellent *Scala Rio* nightclub at Avenida Afranio de Melo Franco 296 in Leblon — one of the largest clubs in town — stages samba shows. Enjoy the mulatto dancers in their glittering carnival costumes. Another major samba performance is that of the group *Oba-Oba*. These mulatto dancers appear at Rua Humaita 110 in Botafogo.

If you have never seen a samba school parade during a carnival, you can sense the atmosphere in a weekly performance by the famous group of *Beija Flor*. This is one of Brazil's best samba schools, and is famous for its colorful parades. The performance takes place at the Morro da Urca, halfway up Sugarloaf Mountain. The performance against the backdrop of the spectacular view is an experience not to be missed.

**Nightclubs:** Rio has a number of excellent clubs, although the very best are for members only and are very expensive. The *Hippopotamus* in Ipanema, on Praça Nossa Senhora da Paz, is a three-story building with an excellent discotheque, a bar, and a very good restaurant.

*Castel* in the Rio Palace Hotel is another excellent and exclusive nightclub. The *Biblos Bar* in Lagoa, Avenida Epitacio Pessoa 1484, is a small, crowded place frequented mainly by singles. Samba shows are held here during the week, and there is dancing on weekends.

On weekends a good discotheque, *Noites Cariocas*, opens its doors at Morro da Urca. Its clientele is mostly young, and the music is mostly Brazilian.

**Bars:** *Cariocas* love to sit in bars, some of which have modest musical shows. Bars proliferate throughout the city, especially in Ipanema, Leblon and Barra.

**Performances:** The best Brazilian musicians often perform in Rio; check the local press for details about forthcoming attractions. These shows are usually very enjoyable experiences: great music, fantastic atmosphere. One of the major performance spots is the *Canecão*, opposite the Rio Sul shopping center. This is a fancy location with prices to match, and the atmosphere is formal and restrained. Things are more lively and open at the *Circo Voador* on Larga da Lapa, downtown.

## Sports

Obviously, the most popular sport in Rio, as in all Brazil, is **soccer**. Every Sunday of the season dozens of thousands of fans stream to the Maracanã stadium for the big game. Soccer fans and others should not pass this up, whether for the game itself or for the atmosphere generated by the crowd. This is particularly true of city derby matches or contests between the best league teams, when the standard of football and the spectator fervor are high.

Another "must" sport while visiting Rio is ocean bathing (see "Beaches" below for details). Rio offers a variety of activities for the sports-minded. Exercise is almost an obsession with the *carioca*, for whom physical fitness and beauty are extremely important. The best of the many sports clubs are at the *Sheraton* and the *Inter-Continental* hotels.

There are **horse races** at the Jockey Club four times a week throughout the year. The Grand Prix is held on the first weekend in August. Horses from all over South America take part, urged on by thousands of spectators.

**Golf** fans will find two clubs in town. Both are private, but they welcome visitors on weekdays: the Gávea Club in São Conrado, opposite the *Inter-Continental Hotel*, and one in Barra da Tijuca.

**Hang gliding** is a well developed sport in Rio, which has one of the best locations in the world for it. Many gliders take off from Pedra Bonita at the top of the Tijuca Forest, and land on the Pepino Beach at the foot of the cliffs. Drive to the launching site by car and enjoy the view, or watch the landing from the beach.

**Motor-racing** is a popular Brazilian sport, and many of the world's leading racing drivers are Brazilian. Each year Rio hosts a Grand Prix race for Formula 1 cars.

For **sailing enthusiasts**, almost all kinds of vessels — from wind-surfers to large yachts — are available for hire at the Gloria Marina. The Rio Yacht Club has a marina of its own, but it is reserved for club members.

Finally, Rio has several ideal surfing beaches (see below).

## Beaches

One of the things everyone does in Rio is visit one of the wonderful bathing beaches which stretch for almost 90 km along the shore. This is the place to which to escape in summer, to enjoy the sun, the cool water, and the crowd. For *cariocas* the beach is almost a second home, and here their good looks are clearly revealed: tanned, lithe men and beautiful, shapely, women whose famous bikinis, reveal much more than they conceal.

On weekends, especially in the summer, the beaches are packed, and it's hard to find a patch of sand. Watching the crowds is fascinating, but this is not the time for a relaxing swim.

The beaches along the bay, at Botafogo and Flamengo, are not particularly clean, and they are used mainly by people living in the close poor northern neighborhoods. The famous **Copacabana beach**, too, has passed its days of glory. Much more popular beaches today are **Ipanema** and **Leblon**. This is where anyone who's anyone turns out to see, and be seen. The eastern end of the Ipanema Beach, the **Praia do Arpoador**, is a good place for surfers or surfer-watchers.

The western end of the **Praia do Pepino** ("cucumber beach"), the end furthest from town, offers several spectator and participant sports; this is the haunt of Rio's motorcyclists, young lovelies, beachcombers, and hang-gliders. The atmosphere is young and easygoing. Beyond is the longest beach in Rio, **Praia Barra da Tijuca**, 15 km long. The highway to this beach is impressive — a double-decker road on pillars that runs parallel to the ocean. Nearer town the beach faces a residential area, and it is, therefore, very crowded on weekends. The further one goes, however, the more deserted the beach becomes. A huge granite boulder marks the end of the long Barra beach and the beginning of another strip 2 km long. After that is a short stretch of beach, only some 150 m in length, called **Prainha**. This lovely place is Rio's best surfing beach, which on weekends attracts many surfers and their companions.

About a half hour drive from Ipanema is the beautiful **Praia Grumari**. On weekdays it is completely deserted, with not a hint of the nearby metropolis. On weekends, *cariocas* flock here for a change of air and scenery.

**Warning:** The sun is very intense during the summer, and those unaccustomed to being out of doors won't manage to adjust during a short visit. Use liberal amounts of protection cream and refrain from extended exposure to the sun. As for swimming in the sea, treat stormy water with caution, even if the surfers make riding the huge waves look like a lot of fun. The great breakers are perilous, and there are lots of whirlpools that cannot be seen from the shore. The human hazards are just as serious. The beaches, particularly the city beaches, crawl with thieves just waiting for an opportunity! Leave your belongings in the hotel, and bring only the minimum amount of money necessary. Leave your cameras behind at the hotel, since these are highly prized loot.

## Weather

Rio is a tropical city. The summer (October-March) is very hot and rainy, with temperatures varying from 32-40°C (90-104°F) with high humidity. Average annual rainfall is over 1000 mm. The Atlantic coast enjoys cooling winds from the ocean, but from Botafogo northwards the heat and humidity are particularly oppressive since this area is on the bay, where the cliffs surrounding the city keep the ocean breezes out. Winter (April-September) is much more pleasant; there are only a few rainy days, and temperatures vary from 20-30°C. (68-88°F).

## Photography

Photo supplies of all kinds are available in Rio, though prices here are high, as they are throughout South America. However, it is possible to find all kinds of film and batteries for cameras. At the lower gallery at Avenida N.S. de Copacabana 581, there is a good, moderately priced selection of photo gear. If you are in the middle of a long trip and have used a lot of film, have it developed in Rio, where the quality of development is high. The best agencies are *Colorcenter* and *Curt*, with branches around town and in the large commercial centers.

## Shopping

In Brazil, only São Paulo surpasses Rio as a place to shop. Apart from the many shops and boutiques throughout town, several large, modern shopping centers have been built in recent years. Rio offers a wide selection of varied products, and it is particularly worthwhile to buy clothing and jewelry here.

Rio is considered to be one of the world's leading cities for **jewelry**. The country's natural resources of gems and precious stones are fully exploited. Jewelers' shops, large and small, are found everywhere. The leader in this field, as previously mentioned, is the international *H. Stern* chain, with its headquarters in Ipanema at Rua Garcia d'Avila 113. The *Natan* chain also has an excellent selection of jewelry and precious stones at reasonable prices, with stores all over the city. Gems are used also in other forms of design, such as statuettes and ashtrays.

Rio also has a good selection of clothing. The casual summer fashions come in a great variety of styles and colors, and prices are low. Footwear and women's handbags are excellent buys, too.

For a wide selection of almost all wares, try the large new shopping centers. One of these is the *Rio Sul* at Avenida Lauro Muller 116, near the Coelho Cintra tunnel in Botafogo. The center consists of four stories of boutiques, shops, restaurants and snack-bars. On the fourth floor is a record store with a good selection of Brazilian music. Other good centers are *Barra Shopping* in Barra (with a skating rink on its lower floor), *São Conrado* in the neighborhood of the same name, and Gávea Shopping Center, on Rua Marquez de São Vicente.

There are other large concentrations of shops and stores all over Rio. For an abundance of exclusive stores with goods of particularly high quality, head for Rua Visconde de Pirajá in Ipanema. Another less expensive shopping area is along Avenida N.S. de Copacabana. Here too the quality of the shops and their goods is high.

## Banks and Currency Exchange

Most Rio banks handle foreign currency exchange and international transactions of all kinds, including cashing travelers' cheques in local currency, for a very small fee. When exchanging currency at the official rate, keep the receipt, so on departure you may reconvert up to one-third of the dollars originally exchanged. While the difference between the official and the "parallel" (black market) rate fluctuates according to the state of the economy, the black market rate is almost always significantly higher. *Casa Piano* on Praça de Paz in Ipanema offers the highest rate of exchange. *Exprinter* is also reliable, and offers good rates at branches throughout the city.

The dollar rate is higher in Rio than anywhere else in Brazil, except for São Paulo. Keep this in mind when changing currency before leaving the city.

## Postal and telephone services
Postal and telephone services in Rio are efficient, and there are many post office branches and telephone offices throughout the city. The branch at Avenida N.S. de Copacabana 540 handles international parcel service. Air mail is recommended; it is more expensive but more reliable than surface mail. This branch also has a telex office.

Not far away, at N.S. de Copacabana 642, is a 24-hour telephone office. There's another one at Rua Visconde de Pirajá 111 in Ipanema, open 6:30am-midnight. There are many other post offices throughout the city. The International Aiport also offers postal, telephone and telex services. Telegrams may be sent from any post office.

## English-language reading material
Brazil has a number of local travel guides in the *Guia Quatro Rodas* series. *Guia Rio* provides important and up-to-date information, and is available at newspaper stands and book stores.

Quite a few good book stores in Rio carry a wide variety of foreign literature, especially in English. Most major hotels also sell English books and newspapers, so finding reading material should not be much of a problem.

The local English daily, *The Latin America Daily Post*, is sold throughout Brazil. The major local journals in Portuguese are *O Globo* and *Jornal do Brasil.*

## Personal security
Social gaps are especially acute in Rio, making the city one of Brazil's major centers of crime. Suffice it to say that for fear of being attacked, local drivers never stop at night, even for a red light. The police are apparently unable to stop crime, even though tourist areas are heavily patrolled. Thus refer to our introduction (see "Personal security") and take all the precautions suggested there. If you nevertheless meet with trouble, do not hesitate to approach the nearest police station or any policeman in the area.

## Important addresses
British Consulate: Praia do Flamengo 284, 2nd Floor, Flamengo.
Tel. 225-7252.
American Consulate: Avenida Presidente Wilson 147, Centro.
Tel. 292-7117.
Immigration Office: Avenida Venezuela 1, Centro.
Tourist Police: Avenida Humberto de Campos 315, Leblon. Tel.
259-7048.
Tourist Bureaus: *Embratur*, Rua Mariz e Barros 13, Praça da
Bandeira. Tel. 273-9592.
*Riotur*. Rua São José 90, Centro. Tel.
232-4320.
24-hour Tourist Information: 580-8000.

# The Rio de Janeiro Carnival
Spectacular carnivals take place throughout Brazil, but the
one in Rio is the most famous. The carnival takes place on
Shrove Tuesday (usually in February) and the three preceding
days. Saturday and Sunday are the days for the procession of
the main samba. The samba school parade, the highlight of
the carnival, with its thousands of dancers, is an unequalled
spectacle, with its electrifying atmosphere and indescribably
exotic and fantastic costumes and decorations. All the clubs in
the city hold special carnival festivities, while passers-by in the
street are drawn into the passing crowds of dancers. All this,
and more, makes Carnival in Rio an unforgettable experience.

### The Samba School Parade
The schools begin preparing for the parade months before the
carnival itself. As the great competition approaches, tension
mounts, preparations become more intensive, and everyone is
absorbed in preparing the stunning decorations and costumes.
During this period, a visit to one of these schools — to watch the
rehearsals and even to take part in the dancing — is fascinating.

Most samba schools are in the distant northern part of town; the
only one in the south is *Beija Flor*, close to the Botafogo beach.
This is one of the largest schools, with a glorious and successful
record in these competitions. *Mangueira*, another large school,
is housed in Palacio do Samba on Rua Visconde de Niteroi,
close to the Maracana Stadium.

**Tickets for the Parade:** Purchasing tickets for the parade is no
simple matter. Officially, tickets are dispensed at *Banerj*, the Rio
de Janeiro State Bank, or at travel agents. However, the supply
runs out within a few days of issue, and then the only way to

*Carnival in Rio de Janeiro — the Samba School Parade*

obtain tickets is from black market dealers who charge several times the official price. Seats are not marked; only the grandstand number appears on the card. The best and most expensive ·of these is No. 11, from which you can see the boulevard itself and the square where the groups finish and disperse. From here one gets a sense of the whole parade. Opposite is Stand No. 4, which is also considered good, although the sun will be in your eyes at dawn. Stands 6 and 13 are cheaper, but one sees only the dispersion square, not the boulevard. Heads of state and VIPs sit in special boxes.

**The Parade:** The major attraction of the Rio Carnival, as we have said, is the competitive parade between the samba schools. A panel of judges grades each school by fixed criteria. The competition lasts two nights, Saturday and Sunday, starting at 7pm and finishing the next day around noon. The first to set out each night are the less well known schools, so there's no need to be overly punctual. Ask locals or inquire at your hotel which are the best groups and in what order they appear. Although the parade is impressive and fascinating, you'll get tired of it sooner or later, so it's worth finding out the best time to attend.

The winning schools are announced at the Maracanazinho Stadium, with the great festivity and exciting atmosphere so characteristic of the carnival as a whole.

On the first Saturday after the carnival, a "Victors' Parade" is held for the four winning groups from each of the two days of competition. Although some of the exuberance and tension of the competition are missing, this, too, will be etched in your memory as an unforgettable event.

## Balls and Parties

Parties abound in nightclubs and private homes. Private parties are, of course, by personal invitation only, but the nightclubs offer a good alternative. There is an entrance fee to the nightclubs which is often steep. Nevertheless, a carnival party should not be missed: crowded, electric, everyone dancing with everyone to nonstop samba music played on wind instruments and drums. The women's costumes leave little to the imagination, and there's no end to the fun.

All nightclubs and discotheques hold these parties; we mention only the largest and most recommended of them.

About a week before the start of the carnival there is a Hawaiian ball in the *Iate Club do Rio de Janeiro* (Rio Yacht Club) in Botafogo. Two days before the carnival, one of the most famous annual events takes place: the Red and Black Ball of the renowned Flamengo soccer team, held at their club, where the revelers dress in the team colors.

Two famous clubs, the *Scala Club* at Avenida Afranio de Melo Franco 292, and *Monte Lebano* on the banks of the Lagoa at Avenida Borges de Medeiros 701, have parties throughout the carnival period. The latter has a particularly magnificent celebration on the last night, called Baghdad Night.

## The Street Carnival

As if the Samba school parade and the parties were not enough, carnival festivities spill into the city streets and beaches. You will meet groups of dancers and musicians celebrating for hours on end. Particularly busy are Avenida Rio Branco downtown, and Avenida Atlantica on the Copacabana beach. Music blares from loudspeakers throughout the evening hours, and thousands are drawn into the whirling throng of merry dancers.

# Around Rio

As if the delights of Rio itself were not enough, the vicinity also has its share of lovely and fascinating places to visit, such as Buzios beach, Itatiaia park with its mountainous jungles and cliffs, colonial-style towns like Angre dos Reis (a memorial to the days of Portuguese rule), and imperial cities established by the l9th-century Brazilian monarchy.

Our tour of the area around Rio is divided into three parts: east along the shore, north to the mountains and the imperial cities, and west along the beautiful coastline between Rio and São Paulo.

## The Coast East of Rio

### Ilha Paquetá

Paquetá island is about an hour and a half by boat from Rio. It is one of the most beautiful islands in Guanabara Bay. There are no motor vehicles on the island, which does much for its tranquil atmosphere. The beaches are marvelous, and strange and varied rocks are strewn in the sand. Few people visit on weekdays, but it is crowded on weekends. To get around, hire a horse or bike.

The ferry to Paquetá leaves every few hours from the quay on Praça 15 de Novembro downtown.

### Niterói

Niterói is on the other side of Guanabara Bay, facing Rio. Founded in 1573, the town has always lived in its big sister's shadow. The 14 km Rio-Niterói is connecting the two cities.

Niterói is a rather nondescript city with a population of around 500,000. Nevertheless, there are some lovely beaches in the vicinity, particularly those facing the ocean. The most beautiful of these are Piratininga, about 20 km away, and Itacoatiara, close by. However, the beaches downtown and those facing the bay are no more beautiful than those on the bay in Rio. Note the beautiful **Igreja Boa Viagem**, built in the l7th century on a small island close to the shore, and **Forte Santa Cruz**, built in 1555, which commands the approaches to the bay.

## SOUTH EASTERN BRAZIL

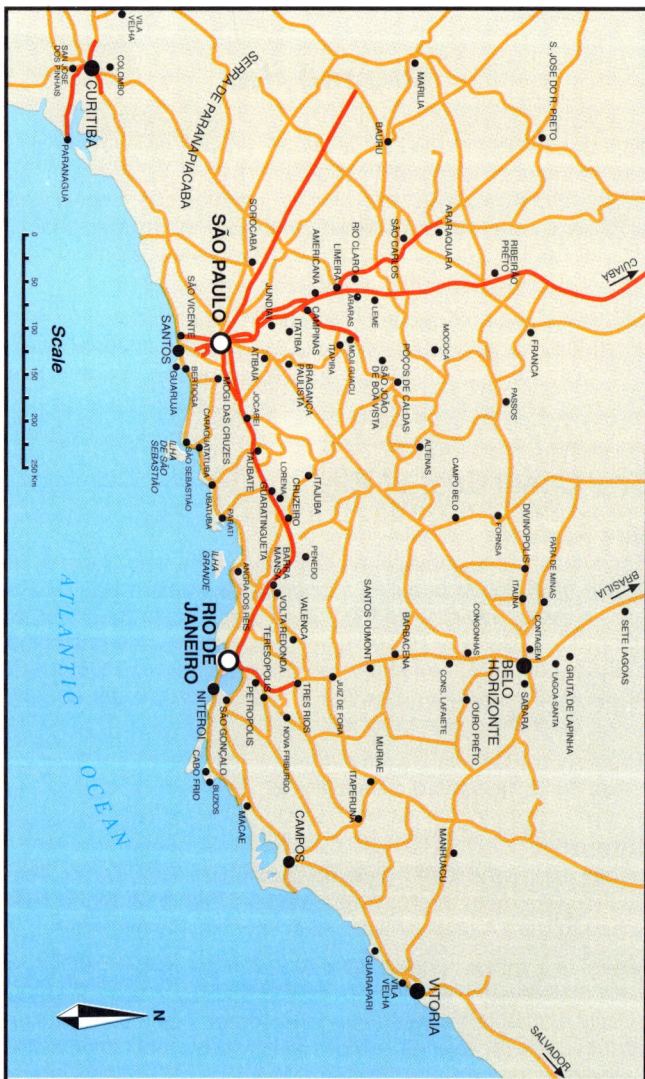

Scale
0
50
100
150
200
250 km

ATLANTIC

OCEAN

SERRA DE PARANAPIACABA

VILA VELHA
COLOMBO
S. JOSE DOS PINHAIS
CURITIBA
PARANAGUA

SÃO JOSE DO RIO PRETO
MARILIA
BAURU
ARARAQUARA
RIBEIRÃO PRETO
CUIABÁ

SOROCABA
RIO CLARO
SÃO CARLOS
AMERICANA
LIMEIRA
ITAPIRA
LEME
MOCOCA
FRANCA
PASSOS

SÃO PAULO
JUNDIAI
ITATIBA
CAMPINAS
MOGI GUACU
POÇOS DE CALDAS
ALTENAS
SÃO JOÃO DE BOAVISTA
CAMPO BELO

SÃO VICENTE
SANTOS
GUARUJA
BERTIOGA
MOGI DAS CRUZES
JACAREI
BRAGANCA PAULISTA
ATIBAIA

CANANEIA
CARAGUATATUBA
UBATUBA
TAUBATE
LORENA
CRUZEIRO
ITAJUBA

ILHA DE SÃO SEBASTIÃO
SÃO SEBASTIÃO
PARATI
PARAITINGUETA
PENEDO

DIVINOPOLIS
FORMIGA
ITAUNA
PARA DE MINAS
SETE LAGOAS
BRASILIA

ILHA GRANDE
ANGRA DOS REIS
BARRA MANSA
VOLTA REDONDA
VALENÇA
SANTOS DUMONT
BARBACENA
CONSELHEIRO LAFAIETE
CONGONHAS
CONTAGEM
BELO HORIZONTE
SABARA
GRUTA DE LAPINHA
LAGOA SANTA

RIO DE JANEIRO
NITEROI
TERESOPOLIS
PETROPOLIS
TRES RIOS
JUIZ DE FORA
NOVA FRIBURGO
OURO PRETO

SÃO GONÇALO
CABO FRIO
BUZIOS
MACAE
CAMPOS
MURIAE
ITAPERUNA
MANHUAÇU

ATLANTIC OCEAN
GUARAPARI
VILA VELHA
VITORIA
SALVADOR

N

*Surroundings of Armação dos Búzios*

Buses for Niterói leave the Rio *rodoviária* every few minutes all day long. There is no point in staying in Niterói overnight.

## Cabo Frio

Cabo Frio is a coastal town of some 75,000. It is about a 3 hours' drive by bus east of Rio. Thanks to its beaches of pure white sand, it has become a popular holiday resort. The town itself is not particularly pleasant, and the hotels are usually rather expensive for the standard and facilities they offer. There is frequent bus service from Rio.

About 18 km from Cabo Frio, is the small town of **Arraial do Cabo**, and in the vicinity are some nice beaches — especially Pontal do Atalaia and Praia Grande. The hotels here are of a lower standard than those in Cabo Frio, but they are much less expensive. There are frequent buses from Cabo Frio to Arraial do Cabo.

## Armação dos Búzios

This delightful little village, 23 km east of Cabo Frio, is surrounded by many beautiful beaches and rocky, green hills that meet the blue sea along a jagged coastline with sandy beaches. This is a popular holiday resort, particularly for rich Brazilians and Europeans, and most of the locals earn a living from tourism. Búzios became very popular with the jet-set after Brigitte Bardot spent a holiday here in the 1960s.

A rather rough dirt road connects Búzios with Cabo Frio. Bus service between the two towns (a one-hour trip) is frequent.

*Area code*: 0246

### Where to stay
Accommodation in Búzios is a rather expensive matter.

*Nas Rocas*: Ilha Rasa; tel. 23-2018, fax 23-1389. About 8 km from Búzios, a very expensive hotel, offering everything a hotel of this category can give.
*Auberge de L'Ermitage*: Estr. Baia Formosa; tel. 23-1103. On the splendid Formosa Beach, about 6 km from the village. You can make your reservations in Rio, tel. 232-0478.
*Pousada dos Buzios*: Av. Jose Benta Dantas 21; tel. 23-1155.
*Pousada Byblos*: Morro do Humaita; tel. 23-1162.

### Where to eat
*Le Streqhe*: Av. Dantas 201, Italian cooking, closed on Mondays.
*Au Cheval Blanc*: Av. Dantas 181; tel. 23-1445. French cuisine, reserve in advance; closed on Tuesdays.

You can find many inexpensive restaurants serving generous portions of fish.

# The Mountain Area

## Itatiaia Park
Some 170 km west of Rio, a little to the north of the highway to São Paulo, is Itatiaia Park with its towering green mountains, rivers, and waterfalls. The highest of its peaks is Agulhas Negras, 2797 m above sea level. Many trails lead to various attractions in the park, through thick foliage and along streams. The most beautiful waterfalls (*cachoeira* in Portuguese) are the Moromba and the Veu Noiva. For trail and camping ground information and maps, stop at the office at the entrance. There is also an interesting museum with specimens of indigenous plants and wildlife.

Near the park is a town of the same name, with several hotels — all rather expensive.

## Petropolis

The most interesting of the mountain towns is Petropolis, some 840 m above sea level. Founded in 1857, it is named after the Emperor of Brazil, Dom Pedro II, who moved the royal residence here and made it the local capital. Today, despite a population of almost 300,000, Petropolis maintains its tranquil, small-town atmosphere. The climate is pleasant, and there are nice views across the verdant hills and mountains.

*Area code*: 0242

### How to get there

Petropolis, 66 km from Rio de Janeiro, is reached by a breathtakingly beautiful route which winds up the hillsides through enchanting forests and along the edges of steep cliffs. The trip takes about an hour and a half, and bus service is frequent throughout the day. Buses from São Paulo reach the downtown terminal.

### Where to stay

*Casa do Sol*: On the road to Rio; tel. 43-5062.
*Retiro*: Rua Raul de Leone 109, tel. 42-0434. Inexpensive and pleasant.

### Where to eat

*Mauricio*: Rua 16 de Março 154; tel. 43-2003. A good fish restaurant.
*Naturalmente*: Rua do Imperador 288; vegetarian cooking.

All along the main street (rua do Imperador), there are plenty of restaurants and snack-bars where tourists on any budget can eat well.

### Tourist services

The Petrotur office is on Praça Rui Barbosa.

### What to see

An obelisk on Rua do Imperador marks the center of town. As mentioned, Dom Pedro II moved the royal residence here in 1845, and had a magnificent royal palace built. Today, it houses the **Museu Imperial**. The museum, on Avenida 7 de Septembro near the obelisk, displays the royal jewels, weapons, clothing, and furniture. One of the most interesting exhibits is the royal crown — with its 639 diamonds and 77 pearls, it weighs 1,720 grams!

The palace is well preserved, and in order to prevent damage to the delicate wooden flooring, visitors are asked to wear overshoes provided at the entrance. The palace is surrounded

*Itatiaia Park*

by a beautiful and well tended garden. (Open Tues.-Sun. noon-5pm, closed Mon.).

Return to the boulevard, turn right, and continue to **Catedral São Pedro**, an impressive Gothic church. Dom Pedro II, his wife Teresa-Christina, and Princess Isabel are interred in magnificent tombs in a room to the right of the entrance.

The front end of the church faces a broad, green boulevard, Avenida Koeller. A stream flows through the center of the boulevard, and on either side are the splendid homes of the local aristocracy. The first house on the right was used by Princess Isabel just before the turn of the century. The beautiful boulevard ends at Praça Rui Barbosa, where *Petrotur* has its offices. Close by is Casa Santos Dumont, which was the summer home of the famous aviation pioneer. Today it houses a modest museum with documents, awards, and other milestones of his life. Avenida Silveira branches off from Praça Barbosa; we follow it to its end and turn right. To the left of the stream, which we have followed all the way from the obelisk, is the **Palacio de Cristal**. This unusual building was erected in 1884 as a pavilion for an international flower show.

The city is surrounded by green hills. You can reach the summit of one of the peaks by cablecar, and here you can enjoy a lovely view and some good mountain air. A long slide provides a novel way of descending to the foot of the hill.

Several kilometers out of town is a well tended golf course, beautifully situated, with a fine view.

## Teresopolis

In the first half of the 19th century, a wealthy Englishman bought a huge area of land in the mountains, and established a house and farm there. In 1855 the government of Brazil bought the farm, divided the land into small estates, and sold it very cheaply to encourage settlement in the region. This place, Empress Teresa Christina's favorite summer resort, gained momentum and rapidly grew into a town which today has a population of some 130,000. At 910 m above sea level, it is the highest of the mountain towns, and many of Rio's wealthy citizens have weekend or summer homes here.

Teresopolis is close to the Serra dos Oragãos (Organ Mountains), so called because the peaks are reminiscent of organ pipes. The range has been declared a national park, and many visitors come here on weekends to stroll along lovely trails through luxuriant vegetation, rivers, waterfalls, and tall cliffs, which are scaled by rock climbers. The most famous of these peaks is called **Dedo de Deus** (the Finger of God) — a high and mighty cliff pointing towards heaven. Its peak, some l650 m above sea level, is visible from several miles away, as one approaches the town.

The road connecting Rio to Petropolis and Teresopolis is stunningly beautiful. The trip takes two hours, and there is a frequent bus service.

### Where to stay

*Rosa dos Ventos*: about 27 km on the road to Nova Friburgo; tel. 742-8833. First class.
*São Moritz*: 36 km on the road to Nova Friburgo; tel. 742-4360, fax 741-1115. A very nice spot.
*Alpina*: Av. pres. Roosevelt 2500; tel. 742-5252. A good establishment, about 3 km from the center of town, moderate prices.

In the center itself are other intermediate-class hotels. The Teresopolis area is well provided with campgrounds, including two in the Serra dos Orgãos.

## Nova Friburgo

This city, in a green and pleasant valley some 850 m above sea level, was founded in 1918 by Swiss immigrants from the town of Fribourg. The population today stands at 160,000, and the main sources of income are light industry and tourism.

From Praça dos Suspiros a cablecar climbs to the top of the Morro da Cruz, providing a fine view of the town and its environs. The cable car runs on weekends from 9am-6pm, and during the week from 1pm. The Olifas park, with its opulent gardens and natural pools, is also well worth visiting.

There are regular buses to Nova Friburgo from Rio (about 140 km) and from nearby Petropolis and Teresopolis.

# From Rio to São Paulo Along the Coast

Two roads link Rio to São Paulo. One is the main highway, on which the trip takes 6 hours. It is a wide, convenient freeway running between green mountains near Park Itatiaia. The second route runs along the coast to Santos, near São Paulo, and is splendidly beautiful — soaring mountains covered in vegetation, slopes spilling into the blue sea, and beaches hidden in sparkling bays. A good road was recently built from Rio to the town of São Sebastião. From São Sebastião to Bertioga, further west, there is still no paved road, but the scenery is extremely beautiful.

The route is lined with little picturesque towns; some are tourist centers for people in the two large cities and outsiders in search of recreation.

### Transportation

Rio and Santos are linked by direct buses which use the local road and take longer to make the trip than they would on the freeway. Many buses link the coastal towns along the way.

### Angra dos Reis

This small, placid town of some 90,000 is 154 km west of Rio. Founded in 1502, it is one of Brazil's oldest settlements. Its little port handles cargoes and serves the fishing boats, while its lovely lagoon and gorgeous beaches make it a popular resort. Boats set out from here several times a week for the 90-minute cruise to Ilha Grande (see below).

Area code: 0243

### Where to stay

*Portogalo*: 26 km away from town on the road to Rio; tel. 65-1022, fax 65-0947.

*Do Frade*: 33 km from town, on the road to Ubatuba; tel. and fax 65-1212. Both hotels have the usual facilities, and you can reserve places before leaving Rio (tel. 267-7375).
*Londres*: Rua Raul Pompeia 75; tel. 65-0112. Inexpensive.
*Palace*: Rua Carvalho 275; tel. 65-0032.

## Ilha Grande
Ilha Grande is an island within the bay of Angra dos Reis. On the sizable island there are lovely beaches, luxuriant tropical vegetation, streams and many waterfalls. Most of the people on the island are either fishermen, who live in little villages, or prisoners... one of Brazil's largest penitentiaries is found on the island.

Boats set out for the island several times a week from Angra dos Reis. A daily boat travels from **Mangaratiba**, a little town on the road from Rio to Angra dos Reis. The cruise to the island takes about an hour and a half. The island has two rather expensive hotels and an abundance of camping grounds. There are also several little restaurants which, of course, serve seafood.

## Parati
This town is about halfway between Rio and São Paulo, 100 km from Angra dos Reis. In the 17th century it was an important port, from which much of the gold discovered in Minas Gerais was shipped out. Seven forts defended the city approaches against pirates. In the 18th century, Parati turned into a center of the slave trade. The Turks and Lebanese who had settled here helped in its development. In the middle of this century, the town center was declared a national monument. Closed to vehicular traffic, it has been preserved as a museum of Portuguese colonial architecture.

The churches in Parati were built with racial segregation in mind — separate facilities for Blacks, Indians and Whites. Only one church was set aside for them all, so as to signify the equality of all people before God... Today, Parati is a popular tourist destination, and many young people come here to spend their vacations on the lovely beaches around the town by day, and in the bars by night.

Area code: 0243

### Where to stay
*Pousada Pardieiro*: Rua do Comercio 74, tel. 71-1370, fax 71-1139.
*Coxixo*: Rua do Comercio 362; tel. 71-1460.

### Where to eat
*Do Hiltinho*: Rua Deodoro 233; tel. 71-1432. Fish.
*Galeria do Engenho*: Rua da Lapa 18; tel. 71-2115. Low priced, serves good portions of fish and seafood.

## Ubatuba
The lovely seaside town of Ubatuba is 75 km from Parati. The little town has a population of about 40,000, of whom many make a living by tourism. Thanks to the many gorgeous beaches in its immediate vicinity, Ubatuba has become a very popular resort, frequented by throngs of the wealthy citizens of Rio and São Paulo.

Especially beautiful beaches are Itamambuca, 12 km north of Ubatuba; Promirim, 23 km away (with natural water pools); the adjacent Vermelha do Sul and Tenorio, a few kilometers south of town; and Enseade and Toninhas, about 10 km south.

Tourists can take to the skies in a light plane for a flight over the jagged green coastline of the area. For details, contact the aviation club (*Aeroclube*, tel. 322-737).

### Where to stay
*Sol e Vida*: Praia da Enseada; tel. 42-0188. First class.
*Mediterraneo*: Praia da Enseada; tel. 42-0112, fax 42-0535. Expensive.
*Ubatuba Palace*: R. Domiciano 500; tel. 32-1500. Expensive.
*Saveiros*: Praia do Lazaro; tel. 42-0172.

There are no inexpensive hotels in the Ubatuba Area, but several tourists can share the rent of a house or an apartment, at lower cost than hotel accommodation. Another option is camping at one of the many camping grounds found in this vicinity.

### Where to eat
Restaurants in Ubatuba are mediocre; expect no culinary surprises. Most of the restaurants specialize in seafood, but there is one good Italian restaurant, *La Mama*, at Avenida Iperoig 332.

## São Sebastião
This is the last stop on the new coastal highway from Rio; the next stretch to the southwest, toward Santos, is in bad condition. Around this little resort town are beautiful beaches, from which ferries set out very often to the island of São Sebastião, better known as Ilhabela.

## Ilhabela

This is also the name of the major town on this lovely island, which is settled on its western or mainland side. Its origin is volcanic; it is covered with thick tropical vegetation and criss-crossed by streams and waterfalls. Hike into the gorgeous scenery, on paths that wind through the thicket and open onto observation points in the soaring mountains, which reach 1300 m in elevation. There are gushing waterfalls, and you can of course swim on one of the beautiful beaches on the island. The beaches on the side facing the mainland are easily accessible by a coastal bus. Another road on the island heads east, to the enchanting Baia de Castelhanos.

The island is accessible by frequent ferries from São Sebastião (a 15-minute cruise). The ferries also carry cars.

### Where to stay

*Itapemar:* Av. Pedro de Paula Morais 341; tel. and fax 72-1329. Best in the island.
*Ilhabela:* Av. Pedro de Paula Morais 151; tel. 72-1083, fax 72-1031. Very good.
*Da Praia:* Av. Pedro de Paula Morais 578; tel. 72-1218. Moderate.
*São Paulo:* R. Doutor Carvalho 46; tel. 72-1158. Inexpensive.

The next stretch of the way, west to Santos, is extremely beautiful. A considerable section of the road as far as the town of Bertioga is unpaved. After Bertioga, one crosses a river by ferry to the island of Guaruja.

## Guaruja

The road from Rio to Santos ends at the resort town of Guaruja (the trip is completed by ferry). The town is situated on an island of the same name, and has a population of 200,000. Its economy is based on tourism and recreaction, and the beaches and streets are well tended and immaculately clean. Many *Paulistas* (inhabitants of São Paulo) have summer homes here, and there are plenty of hotels on the shore. On weekends the town is packed with recreationers, mainly from São Paulo, who fill the Guaruja and Pitangueiras beaches downtown. Many young people spend their days on the beach and their nights at the bars and other entertainment spots. Bear in mind that the roads to São Paulo are packed at the end of the weekend. North of the town are many beaches, of which the nicer are Pernambuco, Iporanga, and Enseada. Some of Guaruja's best hotels are found at Enseada.

### How to get there

Buses from São Paulo reach the Guaruja terminal very

frequently, covering the 87 km at a rapid pace. Buses also arrive from Rio, São Sabastião, and Ubatuba. Santos and the island of Guaruja are linked by many ferries. The ferries, like the road to São Paulo, are packed on weekends; even if they set out every few minutes, drivers waiting in line for a place aboard need a great deal of patience. Take a local bus to the ferry and spare yourself this ordeal.

### Where to stay

Guaruja has plenty of hotels, but few for those on a limited budget.

*Casa Grande*: Av. Miguel Stefano 999; tel. 86-2223. You can make your reservations from São Paulo (tel. 282-4277).
*Delphin*: Av. Miguel Stefano 1295; tel. 86-2111. Slightly less expensive than the Casa Grande.
*Gavea*: Al. Peixoto 311; tel. 86-2212. Pleasant, overlooking the beach and well located, but rather moderate in quality.

### Where to eat

The coastal boulevard, Avenida Miguel Stefano, is lined with many restaurants, all rather expensive. Here, too, are most of the bars and entertainment spots. They are packed, especially on summer weekends.

## Santos

Almost half of all Brazil's imports and exports pass through Santos (pop. 500,000), São Paulo's port city. Its buildings are large, and its avenues wide and verdant. The city does not have any sites of particular interest to tourists, and the beaches are crowded and dirty. The city is built on an island, linked to the mainland by a number of bridges.

The seaside hotel district, where Santos' night life is concentrated, is called Gonzaga. A bus terminal near the city center provides very frequent service to São Paulo. The road between the two cities is an excellent dual carriage road, winding between green mountains; and parts of it are double decker. On weekends, it is congested with traffic from São Paulo heading for recreation on the beaches of Santos and Gonzaga.

From the *rodoviaria*, several buses set out every day on the beautiful coastal highway heading for Rio de Janeiro. There are very frequent buses to São Paulo and there is also an inexpensive, rapid taxi service.

# São Paulo

This city — the largest in South America, with 11 million inhabitants — is Brazil's most important industrial and commercial center, and supplies some 40% of the republic's total production.

São Paulo was founded in 1554 by two Jesuit priests. The mission they set up was just a small, and peaceful town. But since the second half of the last century, it started to develop at an astonishing rate, as its energetic inhabitants built up flourishing industries. In 1920, the population was only half a million, it grew to more than three million by the middle of the century, and in the second half of the 20th century another eight million residents have been added! Today São Paulo is a cosmopolitan city, home to immigrants from many different countries and cultures: Japanese, Italians, Jews, Arabs, and others. Each group clusters in its own neighborhoods and preserves its characteristic lifestyle.

São Paulo does not have any special attractions for the visiting tourist. The view from the air is very impressive, with the city stretching from horizon to horizon, traversed by boulevards and expressways. On the ground, however, the city is gray, graceless, noisy and crowded. Despite its size, São Paulo has hardly any impressive tourist sites. It does, however, have a fairly rich cultural life, and an exciting nightlife. São Paulo is a major business center, and its residents — *Paulistas* — are known for their practicality.

São Paulo has a fine geographical location. The city lies on a plateau 760 m above sea level, and enjoys a relatively pleasant and temperate climate for Brazil: temperatures are lower than usual for the coast, and the humidity is not high.

There is no city center as such in São Paulo. Since all parts of the city are bustling and developing rapidly, new centers make their appearance from time to time, with office buildings, banks, and shopping centers. The old center is the area between Praça da Republica and Praça da Se, where the major offices, banks, and stores are concentrated. The Avenida Paulista and its environs, formerly a prestigious residential neighborhood, has also become a dynamic business center. Most foreign

*São Paolo — aereal view*

consulates are located here. Another fast developing center is Avenida Brigadeiro Faria Lima.

Area code: 011

## How to get there

**By air:** As befits a city of its size, São Paulo has three airports: **Viracopos**, situated 97 km from the center of town, dealing with international traffic as well as domestic flights to Rio and Vitoria; **Congonhas** (only 14 km from downtown), handles most domestic flights, including the Rio de Janeiro shuttle; and **Cumbica/Guarulhos**, the newest and busiest, 30 km from town, handles the heaviest international and domestic flights.

**By land: Buses** - there are two *rodoviarias* (bus depots) in the city. The more important and modern one is Tiete, the terminal for service to all parts of Brazil, as well as for international lines to Montevideo (Uruguay), Asuncion (Paraguay), Buenos Aires (Argentina) and Santiago de Chile. A bridge connects a spacious terminal to the Metro station, on a line to downtown São

*The downtown*

Paulo. The other bus terminal is in Jabaguara, at the southern end of the Metro line. It has very frequent bus service to Santos and to the coast.

The **train** station, Luz, has service to Campo Grande and Corumba, and to Brasília via Campinas.

## Urban transportation

Taking into account its size, public transportation within São Paulo is reasonably good.

**Taxis:** The meter reading has to be translated into the fare according to the driver's charts. São Paulo has three types of taxis: regular taxis; roomy, air-conditioned taxis, which cruise near the major hotels and airports; and radio-linked cabs, which can be ordered by telephone round the clock (tel. 251-1733).

Only one **Metro line** has been completed. A number of other lines are open only over certain stretches. Despite this limitation, the Metro certainly helps ease traffic congestion. All the lines pass through downtown, meet at Praça da Se, and extend to the interurban bus and train terminals. City buses stop at all the Metro stations.

**City buses** serve all parts of the city. But given the distance involved, a bus trip is liable to take a long time.

Whichever means of transportation you use to get around the city, try not to travel during the rush hours — around 8am, noon, and 6pm — when traffic is heavy, slow, and congested.

## Where to stay

*Maksoud Plaza*: Al. Campinas 150; tel. 251-2233, fax 251-4202. The best in town, and the most expensive.
*Hilton*: Av. Ipiranga 165; tel. 256-0033, fax 257-3137. Well located.
*Ca'd'Oro*: R. Augusta 129; tel. 256-8011, fax 231-0359. Superb Italian restaurant.
*Othon Palace*: R. Libero Badaro 190, tel. 239-3277, fax 239-1227. High standard, less expensive than the former.
*Excelsior*: Av. Ipiranga 770; tel. 222-7377, fax 222-8369. Moderately priced.
*Plaza Maraba*: Av. Ipiranga 757; tel. 220-7811.
*Samambaia*: R. 7 de Abril 422; tel. 231-1333.
*Lider*: Av. Ipiranga 908; tel. 223-5455. Cheap.
*Itamarati*: Av. Vieira de Carvalho 150; tel. 222-4133. Inexpensive.

Young tourists, especially those with limited budgets, will find many moderately priced hotels around the Luz terminal, especially along Rua Santa Ifigenia. Most of the hotels here are cheap, although some are slightly more expensive. Check a number of these hotels before selecting one that suits your budget and requirements.

## Where to eat

In a town like São Paulo, you have all the chances to find all kind of restaurants, covering the span from the traditional to the exotic, and from the expensive to the cheap. As usual, downtown you can find popular places, serving economic dishes, and the fast-food empires.

*Mandalun*: al. Itu 1564; tel. 282-8136. Closed on Mondays. Arabian dishes.
*Hong Sheng*: Rua Santa Cruz 630; tel. 549-3059. Modest place, but great Chinese food.
*Wessel Grill*: Rua Bela Cintra 1855; tel. 280-9107. Very good barbecues.
*Los Molinos*: Rua Vasconcelos Drumond 526; tel. 215-8211. Superb Spanish cuisine.

*Le Coq Hardy*: Av. Adolfo Pinheiro 2518; tel. 246-6013. Closed on Sundays, expensive and still worth. French restaurant.
*Massimo*: Al. Santos 1826; tel. 284-0311. Highly recommended, even if Italian pasta is not your dish. Closed on Sundays.
*Jardim de Napoli*: Rua Dr. Domenico Prado 463; tel. 66-3022. Closed on Mondays, excellent Italian food.

At the turn of the 19th century, and the first half of the twentieth, Brazil attracted a great number of immigrants from all over the world, among them Japanese. The large nippon community can be seen mainly in the **Liberdade** quarter. The streets on that district are packed with Japanese restaurants. Some have no tables, and diners sit on mats. If you like this type of food, go to the following:

*Suntory*: Al. Campinas 600; tel. 283-2455.
*Komazushi*: Av. Brig. Luis Antonio 2050; tel. 287-1820.
*Mel*: Rua Araujo 75; tel. 257-5550. Naturist, downtown.

## Tourist services
The **São Paulo Tourist Office**, *Paulistur*, has set up tourist information booths throughout the city. There is a booth at Praça da Republica (Open Mon.-Fri. 9am-6pm, Sat. noon-4pm, Sun. 9am-1pm). Another such booth is found at the Liberdade Metro station, and keeps the same hours. There are also booths at the Se Metro station (Open Mon.-Fri. 9am-6pm, and weekends 9am-1pm), on Praça Dom José Gaspar, on Avenida Paulista, and on Avenida Ipiranga.

All the airlines that fly to Brazil have offices downtown. *Varig* has branch offices throughout the city, and at Congonhas airport.

**Car rental:** There are many rent-a-car companies in São Paulo. A number of companies, such as *AFM* and *Crasso*, can provide chauffeured cars. Black-Tie has a fleet of Cadillacs, for those intent upon leaving plenty of dollars in Brazil. The large rent-a-car companies are *Nobre*, *Hertz*, *VIP's*, and *Locabraz-Avis*. But be warned: city traffic is unbearable, and driving around town will turn you into a nervous wreck. Don't rent a car unless you plan on using it for excursions out of town.

## Tourist sites
São Paulo's densely packed old center spreads between Praça da Republica and Praça da Sé. **Praça da Republica** is a spacious green square, the site of a beautiful handicraft market on Sundays. The **Edificio Italia** rises skyward at the corner of Avenida São Luis, and the observation deck at the top affords the best view of the giant city. Most of the adjacent streets are

## SÃO PAULO

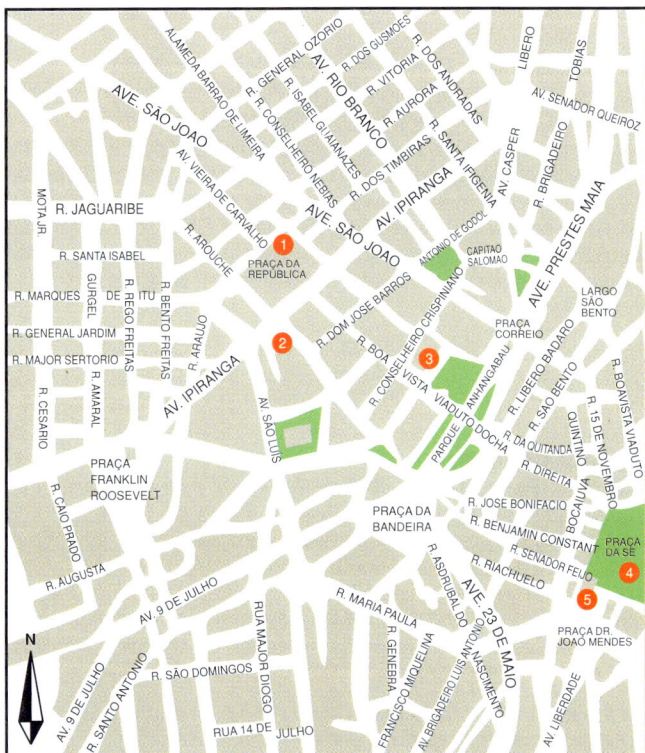

closed to automotive traffic, and have an enormous number of stores and inexpensive restaurants.

There are guided tours of the **Municipal Theater**, on Praça Ramos Azevedo, on Wednesdays and Fridays, 12-1pm and 2-3pm. Work on this magnificent building began in 1903. It was

*Milking a snake for venom at the Instituto Butantan*

enlarged, in the 1950s, its main auditorium can hold almost 2000 spectators. **Praça da Sé** is a large square, with a row of fountains that are illuminated at night. The large Gothic-style **Catedral Metropolitana** (Municipal Cathedral) faces on to this square.

Time has transformed the **Avenida Paulista**, formerly the city's prestigious residential sector, into a bustling commercial district. Most of the foreign consulates are located here. Southwest of the avenue is the pleasant and peaceful **Jardim America** neighborhood. São Paulo's most important art museum, the **Museu de Arte de São Paulo** (MASP), is situated at Avenida Paulista 1578 (open Tues.-Fri. 1pm-5pm; weekends 2pm-6pm; closed on Mondays; tel. 251-5644). The modern building holds a permanent exhibit of the works of European artists, and Brazilian art is somewhat scarce. This situation is redressed by the two museums of modern art — the **Museu de Arte Contemporânea**, and the **Museu de Arte Moderna**, both situated in the **Parque do Ibirapuera**. This large park has other museums, of which the most noteworthy are the **Museum of Folklore**, with exhibits of traditional costumes, household implements, and musical instruments (open Tues.-Sat. noon-6pm, Sun. 10am-6pm; tel. 572-5353); and the **Museu Aeronautica** (Aeronautical Museum), housed in the same building, which commemorates the work of aviation pioneers (open Tues.-Fri. 2pm-5pm; weekends 10am-5pm; tel. 570-3915. Currently closed). A large sculpture in honor of the city's pioneers graces the entrance to the park.

One of São Paulo's most popular sites is the **Instituto Butantan** (Butantan Institute), at Avenida Vital Brasil 1500. The institute, founded in 1898 and affiliated with the Ministry of Health of São Paulo State, carries out various research projects in health and biology. It gained fame by specializing in snakes and poisonous animals. The institute has one of the largest and most impressive collections of snakes in the entire world — tens of thousands of snakes, both poisonous and non-poisonous. Several times a day you can watch the venom being milked from the snakes. Be sure to visit the museum, near the entrance to the institute, where there is an exhibit of several poisonous creatures, and methods of protection against them (open Tues.-Sun., 9am-5pm, tel. 813-7222).

Of further interest to animal lovers are the **Zoological Gardens**, about half an hour's trip from the center of town, with a very large and interesting collection of animals from all over the world. Another interesting visit for animal lovers is the **Simba Safari**, not far from the zoo.

## Entertainment
São Paulo offers a wide variety of entertainmment, not concentrated in a single district, but spread throughout the giant city. The magnificent **Teatro Municipal** (Municipal Theater), located downtown, stages concerts, shows, and operas. Movie theaters — usually modern and comfortable — are scattered all over town. São Paulo has many night clubs, such as the *Ta Matate*, in the Itaim neighborhood, and the *Pool Music House*, a dance club, usually jammed with throngs of gyrating youths. The southern end of Rua Augusta and its cross-streets have many bars, frequented mainly by young people and students. These places are especially crowded at weekends.

For children, young people, and the young in spirit, São Paulo's amusement park, the *Playcenter*, will provide a happy diversion. The most exciting attraction is the huge roller coaster. Another attraction is *Cine 2000*, which shows 3-D movies that give the spectator the sensation of being right in the middle of the action. The Playcenter is on Avenida Marginal do Tiete (Open Tues.-Fri. 2pm-10pm, Sat. 2pm-11pm, Sun. 10am-10pm.)

## Shopping
Since it is Brazil's largest commercial center, São Paulo is undoubtedly the place to do your shopping. In recent years a number of large and modern shopping centers have been built. The most impressive and highly recommended of these (not just to visit) is *Eldorado*, located rather far out in Pinheiros, and noted for its interesting, modern architecture. This gigantic shopping center has cafes, restaurants, stores, fun arcades, and very expensive boutiques. The *Iguatemi* shopping center is not far away. Another large shopping center is *Ibirapuera*, near the park of the same name. Here, too, there are numerous stores and boutiques, where prices are lower than in the other shopping centers. Along Rua Augusta, particularly in the garden distric, the *Jardims*, there are many luxury shops and boutiques. Many clothing stores and shops selling imported goods are concentrated downtown, and their prices are usually low.

## Postal and telephone services
The São Paulo telephone company, *Telesp*, provides good and efficient service. You will have no trouble calling anywhere in the world. A telephone office at Avenida 7 de Abril 295, downtown, is open round the clock. Other downtown telephone offices are found at: Praça Dom José Gaspar 22, Rua Benjamin Constant 200, and Rua Martins Foate 150, (all three open daily, 6:30am-10:30pm). There are also telephone offices throughout the city, including one at the Luz terminal and one at Congonhas airport.

Numerous post offices are scattered throughout the city. There is one at Congonhas airport, another downtown, at Praça da Republica 390, and another in the Ibirapuera shopping center.

## Banks and currency exchange
Most Brazilian banks have offices downtown, and most bank branches buy foreign currency. If you want to buy local currency on the black market, there are quite a few *casas-de-cambio* (money exchanges) downtown, especially near Praça da Republica. Exprinter, at Rua Itapetininga 243, is good and reliable.

## Important addresses
American Consulate: Jardim America, Rua Presidente João Manuel 933 (tel. 881-6511).
British Consulate: Cerqueira Cesar, Avenida Paulista 1938, 17th (tel. 287-7722).
Tourist Office (*Paulistur*): Avenida Olavo Fontoura 1209 (tel. 26-2122).

**Emergency Numbers:**
Ambulance: tel. 136
Police emergency: tel. 190.
Police downtown station: tel. 222-8386.

# Southern Brazil

Southern Brazil has a different character from the rest of the republic. This is the most developed part of the country, where European influence is particularly strong. The population is mainly made up of descendants of immigrants, chiefly German and Italian. This area has the lowest illiteracy rate in the entire country. Agriculture is developed, the land is rich and fertile, and yields are good. The local wine industry, especially that of the southermost province state of Rio Grande do Sul, is justly famous. The other two southern states are Santa Catarina and Parana.

The green mountain range known as Serra do Mar, which never exceeds 1000 m above sea level, runs parallel to the coast. Its western slopes gradually become a broad and rolling plateau, which extends to the western borders of southern Brazil. The climate is fairly pleasant, but chilly in winter. One of Brazil's most important tourist sites is the Iguaçu Falls, which are at the western edge of this region.

## Curitiba
Curitiba, founded at the end of the 17th century, is the capital of Parana state. The town lies in an area of green hills, 900 m above sea level. The climate is pleasant and temperate. Curitiba has a population of approximately one million, and is a modern industrial and commercial center, but has no places of special interest. The train ride from Curitiba to Paranaguá is, however, a breathtaking trip.

Area code: 041

### How to get there
The airport, 17 km from the town, is served by many flights from all of Brazil's important towns. The modern new terminal for buses and trains, *Rodoferroviaria*, is not far from downtown. From here, a number of buses leave daily for Rio de Janeiro (about 12 hours), São Paulo (6 hours), Florianopolis (6 hours), Porto Alegre (about 11 hours), and Foz do Iguaçu (about 12 hours), to which there are also night coaches. The *Graciosa* bus company runs frequent buses throughout the day to Paranagua, which is also accessible by train. If you want to travel from

Curitiba to Iguaçu, be sure to buy your bus ticket early in order to guarantee yourself a seat.

## Where to stay
*Bourbon*: Rua Candido Lopes 102; tel. 223-0966, fax 322-2282. Deluxe, in the Centro.
*Duomo Park*: Rua Visconde do Rio Branco 1710, Centro; tel. 225-3545, fax 224-1816. Another very good hotel, centrally located, good value.
*Iguaçu Campestre*: Out of town, 8 km on the road to São Paulo; tel. 262-5313, fax 262-5775. Good motel out of town, with swimming pool.
*Del Rey*: Rua Ermelino de Leão 18, Centro; tel. 224-3033. Moderate, good location.
*Ouro Verde*: Rua Dr. Murici 419; tel. 224-1633.

Cheaper hotels can be found opposite the bus and train terminal, on Av. Afonso de Camargo, and on the small streets that are linked to it.

## Where to eat
*Alpendre*: Rua Visconde do Rio Branco 1046, Centro; tel. 224-5694. Highly recommended Portuguese cuisine.
*Matterhorn*: Rua Mateus Leme 575, Centro; tel. 233-6115. Swiss menu, try the meat fondue.
*Ile de France*: Praça 19 de Dezembro 538; tel. 223-9962. Good French cuisine.
*Green Land*: Praça Garibaldi 18, Centro; tel. 232-3813. Vegeterian, self-service, very modest.
*Pinheirão*: Rua João Negrão 400, Centro; tel. 224-1662. A good rodízio, for meat-eaters.

There are lots of inexpensive restaurants around the train station.

## Tourist sites
Curitiba's modern center teems with life. **Rua 15 de Novembro**, the town's main street, contains the most important banks and office buildings. A section of the street, from Praça Osorio to Praça Generoso Marques, is closed to vehicular traffic. The old Town Hall, built in 1916 in ornate art-nouveau style, is located in this square. Today the building houses the **Museu Paranaense** (Parana Museum) which displays interesting archaeological and anthropological exhibits, as well as artifacts of the Guarani Indians (open Tues.-Fri. 9am-6pm; weekends noon-5pm). Nearby is **Praça Tiradente**, with its impressive cathedral.

A lovely **handicrafts market** is held in Praça Rui Barbosa on Saturdays, where artifacts and handicrafts — especially in ceramics and wood — are sold.

### Vila Velha
Vila Velha is a beautiful national park, some 100 km from Curitiba. Here you can see interesting rock formations, carved by wind and rain. Daily buses reach Vila Velha from Curitiba and São Paulo.

## The train from Curitiba to Paranaguá
Brazil's most beautiful rail route is the one linking Curitiba to the port of Paranaguá. The tracks cross the verdant Serra do Mar range, pass through tunnels, climb mountains, and traverse canyons. All along the route you will see luxurious vegetation, streams, and waterfalls.

There are two daily trains. One, intended for tourists, has particularly comfortable cars and stops en route at especially scenic spots. This train leaves the Curitiba station slightly after 8am, and returns from Paranagua at 3pm. The regular train, which costs about a third of the tourist train, leaves Curitiba at 7am and returns at 4:30pm. The ride to paranaguá takes about three hours.

You can travel one way by train, and return by bus. Buses are much quicker than the train, and also much more frequent.

## Paranaguá
This port town of 110,000 inhabitants lies on Paranaguá Bay. The harbor mainly serves landlocked Paraguay. Visit the quays to watch the bustling activity in the spacious port.

In the town itself, stroll through the area near the coast and the fish market. Apart from these, there are no other places of interest. If you want to go for a swim, you will have to go to Pontal do Sul, about 45 km away. Buses there leave the small bus station frequently.

**Ilha do Mel** is a particularly beautiful island, with enchanting beaches and small fishing villages. You can take an enjoyable hike along the beaches and coves, and sleep in the fishermen's houses. The boat from Pontal do Sul to the island takes about half an hour, and there is no regular departure time.

## Florianopolis
Florianopolis, the capital of Santa Catarina state, has about 250,000 residents. The town is named after Floriano Peixoto, the leader of the federal revolution of 1893. The town has two

*The southern beaches — dense with vegetation and yachts*

parts — one on the island of Santa Catarina, and the other on the mainland. Two large bridges span the 250 m wide strait. The island is lovely, with green hills, blue lakes, and splendid beaches. The place is a popular tourists site, and swarms with foreign tourist and Brazilian vacationers from December to February.

Area code: 0482

## How to get there

Florianopolis' small airport is on the island, about 11 km from the center of town. A number of daily flights link it with Rio de Janeiro, São Paulo, Porto Alegre, and all the other state capitals. There is a daily flight from Foz do Iguaçu. Especially beautiful is the flight from São Paulo, which flies low over the magnificent coastline.

The modern and spacious bus terminal is also on the island, at the foot of the Colombo Sales bridge, the southernmost of the two bridges. Scheduled buses leave for Porto Alegre (about 8 hours), Curitiba (about 6 hours), and São Paulo (about 12 hours). Daily buses also leave for Foz do Iguaçu, Asuncion (Paraguay), and Buenos Aires (Argentina).

## Food and Lodging

*Floraniopolis Palace*: Rua Artista Bittencourt 2; tel. 22-9633. Best of town, near the central square.

*Faial Palace*: Rua Felipe Schmidt 87; tel. 23-2766, fax 22-9435. Good service, better priced than the former.

*Querencia Palace*: Rua Jeronimo Coelho 1; tel. 22-2677. Good and reasonable prices.

*Jureré Praia*: Al. 1, Praia de Jureré; tel. 66-0108. About 25 km from town, deluxe services. Minimum of one week stay (in the high season).

*Canasvieiras Praia*: Rua da Milu 13, praia de Canasvieiras; tel. 66-0310. About 28 km from town, in Canasvieiras; good but crowded and noisy during the tourist season.

Bars and restaurants can be found up and down Avenida Arruda Ramos, which runs along the north coast of the city, where most of the nightlife is centered.

Sea food is the most popular fare in Florianopolis, and for good reason! Throughout the island, and especially along the beaches, lakes, and tourist sites, there are an incredible number of restaurants serving all sorts of fish, crab, shrimp, and other delicacies. Avenida Rendeiras, south of Lake Conceição (see below) is "wall-to-wall" fish restaurants. Noteworthy here is *Alice Maria Vieira*, which serves large and satisfying portions at low prices — the shrimp is excellent.

## Tourist services

The town has a number of **tourist information** bureaus, of which the best and most efficient is on the mainland, near Colombo Sales bridge (open daily 8am-6pm), in front of a small handicrafts shop. Another tourist office is located in the main square, Praça 15 de Novembro (open daily 8am-10pm during the tourist season; open Tue-Fri. 8am-8pm out of season). There are also information bureaus at the airport and the bus terminal, but they are not always helpful.

The *Scuna-Sul* company (tel. 221-860) organizes boat trips in the bays between the island and the mainland. There are two trips — in the northern and southern bays. The cruise in the southern bay, which lasts 8 hours, is recommended.

**Car rental:** Rent-a-car services can be found along Avenida Rio Branco. The largest is *Nobre*, at 110 Rio Branco. Coelho's offices are at the airport.

## Tourist sites

Florianopolis' old section has narrow streets and colonial buildings. In the middle of **Praça 15 de Novembro** stands a huge *Ficus* tree more than a hundred years old. The cathedral, built in 1750, is on the same *Praça*. To the left of the square is **Palacio de Governo** (the State Capitol). On the edge of downtown rises Morro da Cruz hill, which offers a panoramic view of the town and its surroundings. A short bus ride from the center of town takes you to the top.

### Santa Catarina Island
Santa Catarina is an enchanting island, with 42 beaches, green mountains, and gorgeous lakes. In the middle of the island is a beautiful large lake, Lagoa da Conceição. The most beautiful beaches are the eastern ones, which are less developed and wilder than the northern beaches. Praia da Joaquima is one of the most popular beaches, and is packed and noisy during the tourist season. Other good beaches are Campeche and Armação, south of Praia de Joaquima, and Moçambique and Praia dos Ingleses, to the north.

Among the northern beaches Canasvieiras deserves mention — it is another beautiful beach which is jammed during the tourist season. You can reach the eastern part of the island from Florianopolis — local buses cover the distance in about half an hour. The road crosses a narrow bridge, below which anglers cast their lines into the water. Two roads lead to the northern end of the island, one on the west coast and the other on the east coast.

# Rio Grande do Sul
Brazil's southernmost state, Rio Grande do Sul, borders on Uruguay to the south and Argentina to the west. The dominant landscape is pastoral and hilly. The land is extremely fertile, and provides excellent grazing for cattle. The millions of heads of cattle and pigs raised here serve the extensive meat and leather industry. Viniculture has also developed in the area, and about 75% of all Brazilian wine is produced here. The center of the wine industry is **Caxias do Sul**, a modern town of about 300,000 residents, many of whom are the descendants of Italian immigrants. Visit the wine cellars and taste their quality wines.

Many residents of Rio Grande do Sul raise cattle on their carefully tended ranches. These cowboys are known as *gauchos*, and the name has spread and stuck to all the inhabitants of the state. The locals are friendly and hospitable, and will be happy to help out whenever required. Their easy-going manner is apparently influenced by the local climate, which is pleasant and temperate. Only a few summer days are uncomfortably hot, and the winters are no more than cool, while in the mountains snow falls only for a few days a year.

## Porto Alegre

Porto Alegre, the capital of Rio Grande do Sul, has about 1,400,000 residents. The town is developing at a rapid pace. Even though it is modern and fairly busy, it still preserves the charm of bygone years. The city is on the banks of the Rio Guaiba, where the river empties into the largest freshwater lake in South America — Lagoa dos Patos. The lake, which has an outlet to the ocean, is the site of Porto Alegre's main harbor. This serves as the point of export for many goods manufactured in the south — in particular leather, meat, and tobacco products.

Porto Alegre is thus the most important commercial center south of São Paulo. All the same, there's not much to interest tourists here.

The main street — 7 de Setembro, flanked by modern skyscrapers, crosses Rua Canabarro, which has a daily **handicrafts market** famous for its leather goods. The **Mercado Publico** (central market) — built in 1869 — is on Praça 15 de Novembro.

Several public buildings are situated on Praça Deodoro, of which the most important is **Palacio Piratini** (Piratini Palace), which serves as the seat of government. The **cathedral** is next door. It was renovated in 1986, with tiles at the facade and fine renaissance style. Across from these two buildings is the **São Pedro Theater**, constructed in 1858 in baroque style, and renovated in 1984. Near the square, at 1231 Duque de Caxias street, is an interesting historical museum, the **Museu Julio de Castilhos** (open Tues.-Fri. 9am-6pm; weekends 9am-noon and 2-5:30pm). Close by is a spacious park, with lots of greenery and ponds.

Area code: 0512

### Food and Lodging

A number of good and expensive hotels can be found downtown. The best is the *Plaza São Rafael* at Avenida Alberto Bins 514 (tel. 216-100). The hotel has two good restaurants: one is the *Capitão Rodrigo*, which serves good steaks, and *Le Bon Gourmet*, the more elegant one. Moderately priced hotels can be found near the bus terminal.

A good choise for a vegetarian restaurant in the centro is *Associação Macrobiótica*, at Rua Mavechal Floriano 72.

*Floresta Negra* is a very good restaurant serving German cuisine. Av. 24 de Outubro 905 (Moinhos de Vento), tel. 22-7584. For dinner only.

For a very good *rodizio* style *churrascaria*, try *Nova Brésica*, Rua 18 de Novembro 81 (Navegantes), tel. 42-3285.

**Transportation**
Porto Alegre's sprawling airport, 10 km from the center of town, has service to all parts of Brazil. *Varig* flies daily to Foz do Iguaçu, Montevideo (Uruguay), and Buenos Aires (Argentina).

The modern and well-planned bus terminal is not far from downtown. There are many daily buses to Rio (over 24 hours), São Paulo, and Florianopolis (about 6 hours). There is one bus a day to Foz (about 18 hours), and regular service to Montevideo and Buenos Aires (24 hours).

## On to Uruguay and Argentina
The Brazilian border town on the coastal road from Porto Alegre to Montevideo is **Chui**. Two buses a day make the 8-hour trip. Remember to get your passport stamped when leaving Brazil, and again at Chuy, on the Uruguayan side of the border.

Some 650 km west of Porto Alegre is **Uruguaiana**, on the Argentinian border. A bus leaves there every half hour for Paso de los Libres on the Argentinian side, crossing the bridge over the Rio Uruguai, which forms the border between the two countries.

# The Iguaçu Falls

When you see the torrents of water thundering down on all sides, you cannot help being stirred by that feeling of awe one experiences when in the presence of Nature in all her sublimity. The Iguaçu Falls, among the largest and most impressive in the world, are an enthralling experience, an amazing sight of overwhelming height, which gives the abstract words "natural wonder" a real and unforgettable meaning.

Of all the natural wonders and landscapes that South America has to offer the tourist, these gigantic falls, located on the border of Brazil and Argentina, near the common border with Paraguay, are of the most impressive. It is not surprising that they draw more than two million visitors annually. Every second, nearly 450,000 gallons of water come crashing down over a distance of 4 km, in hundreds of subsidiary waterfalls that are 60 to 80 meters high. This magnificent sight, together with the clouds of spray that envelop the area and the incessant roar of the cascading waters, recreates primeval nature in all her glory. And as if to complete the legendary quality of the place, the whole area is covered by a luxuriant tangle of tropical growth, a study in bright green, a feast for the eye.

Area code: 0455

## How to get there
**From Brazil:** There is daily bus service to Foz do Iguaçu (the town on the Brazilian side of the falls) from Rio de Janeiro (travel time: 24 hours), São Paulo (17 hours), and Curitiba (12 hours). The buses are luxurious and the roads are good. The buses leave from the central bus station at all hours of the day and night. You must buy your ticket **at least** one day in advance!

*Cruzeiro do Sul* and *Varig* fly daily from Rio via São Paulo to Foz, and back.

**From Argentina:** The falls are 300 km from Posadas, and many buses run from the Posadas train station to Puerto Iguazu (the town on the Argentinian side of the falls). A train leaves Buenos Aires daily for Posadas. The journey takes about 20 hours, and from there you must continue by bus to the falls. *Expreso Singer* has a direct bus several times a day from Retiro Station to Posadas (20 hours) and on to Puerto Iguazu (4 more hours).

*Aerolineas Argentinas* runs regular and frequent flights from Buenos Aires to Posadas, from which buses leave frequently for Puerto Iguazu. Direct flights to Iguazu, and especially return flights, are heavily booked.

**From Paraguay:** Buses from Asuncion cover the distance to Foz in about seven hours, along Paraguay's only paved highway. The Nuestra Señora, Rapido Iguazu, and Pluma companies run several buses a day to the Brazilian side (Foz) and back. The buses are comfortable and the journey pleasant, usually with one intermediate stop.

## Food and lodging

You have three options: to stay in Puerto Iguazu (Argentina), to stay in Foz do Iguaçu (Brazil), or to stay in Ciudad del Este (Paraguay). Your best bet is Brazil, since it offers the best tourist facilities. So, if you're coming from Brazil, stay there until you continue your journey. If you're coming from Argentina on the way to Brazil, cross the border and stay in Foz. And if you're coming from Asuncion, the same advice holds: cross the bridge to the Brazilian side.

### Foz do Iguaçu (Brazil)

This city of more than 200,000 people is geared entirely to cater to the local and foreign tourists who come to visit the famous falls. Its long avenues and adjacent streets are packed with dozens of hotels of varying quality.

## Where to stay

*Hotel das Cataratas*: Rod. das Cataratas km 28; tel. 74-2666, fax 74-1688. Opposite the falls, superb view.
*Diplomat*: Av. Brasil 278; tel. 73-3155. A walking distance from downtown.
*Foz do Iguaçu*: Av. Brasil 97, tel. 74-4455, fax 74-1775. Cheaper.

Behind the bus station you will find the popular restaurants where you can sit outside and enjoy a good and inexpensive meal.

### Puerto Iguazú (Argentina)

The town has many hostels and hotels of reasonable quality covering all ranges of prices.

*Internacional Iguazú*: Parque Nacional, tel. 20790. The most luxurious and expensive (about U$S 150 a double room with a view to the falls, slightly cheaper if it doesn't), with a swimming pool, casino and an excellent restaurant; situated along the falls.

*Esturión*: Av. Tres Fronteras 650, tel. 20020. Another five-star hotel, in town.
*Cataratas*: Ruta 12, km 4, tel. 21100. Four stars, very good service.
*Alexander*: Av. Córdoba 665, tel. 20633. Three stars.
*Libertador*: P. Moreno y Bonpland (near the bus station), tel. 20416. Three stars.
*Paraná*: Av. Brasil 367, tel. 20399. Very modest, and yet can be recommended.

Near the bus station you can find cheaper arrangements in hostels (*hospedajes* and *hosterías*).

There are also several camping sites nearby; the best is *Pindo*, 1/2 km outside town in the direction of the falls (buses from town to the falls pass by the entrance).

As far as food is concerned, you will not go hungry. All the large hotels have good restaurants — offering both Argentinian and Brazilian cuisine — and there is no shortage of restaurants in town. Behind the bus station you will find the popular restaurants where you can sit outside and enjoy a good and inexpensive meal.

Evening is a good time to visit Ciudad del Este, a city still referred by many as Puerto Stroessner, its former name, with its streets crammed with stores, restaurants, and casinos. Prices here vary according to the changing value of the dollar in the neighboring countries, so that sometimes you will find "bargains" and sometimes everything is outrageously expensive.

## How to tour and what to see
The falls are on the border, but more than 80% of them are in Argentinian territory. The best vantage point, where you can see the entire falls in all their vast splendor, the rich foliage, and the surrounding area, is undoubtedly from the Brazilian side. Every hour, buses marked *Cataratas* or *Parque Nacional* leave the central bus station in Foz for the falls. The journey lasts about 30 minutes; after you have paid you will be let off in front of the luxurious *Hotel das Cataratas*. From here you follow a long, winding path through the dense undergrowth to the heart of the waterfall area, where you can look out over the whole region — a truly breathtaking sight. The most exciting part of the hike is crossing the narrow bridge that leads almost into the heart of the great **Floviano Falls** — and being soaked to the skin by the flying spray. At the bottom of the cliffs is a small elevator to take you back up to the top, from where you can return to the hotel (lunch at its excellent restaurant is highly recommended), and back to town (buses leave once

## *THE IGUAÇU FALLS*

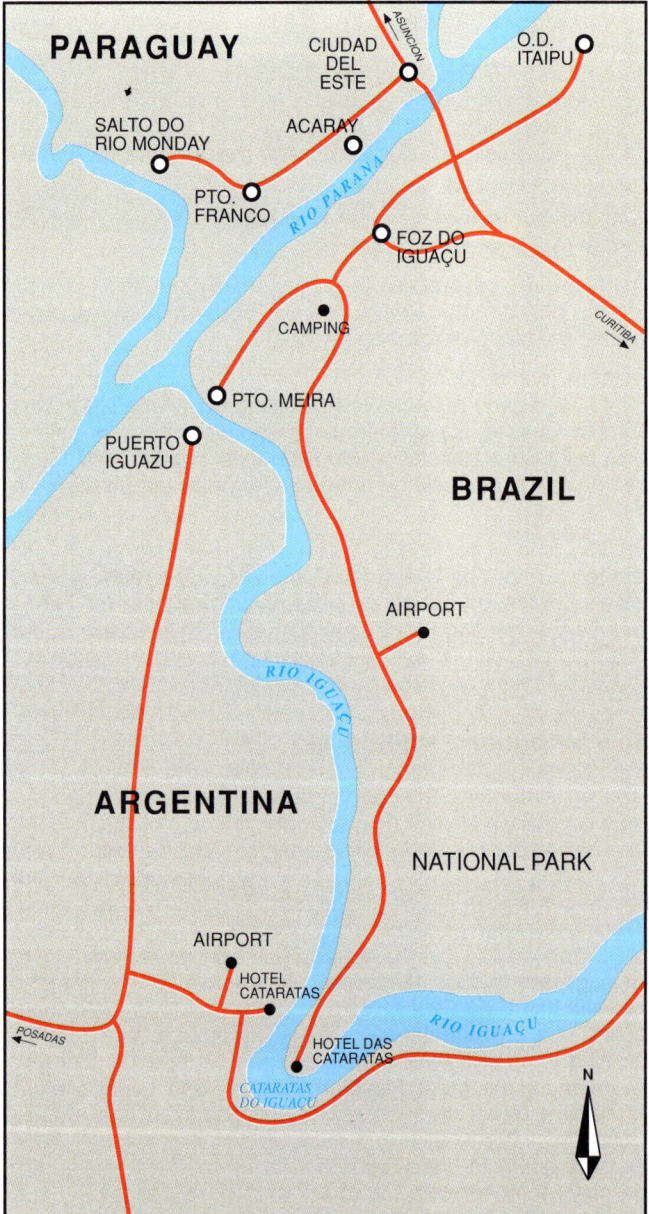

PARAGUAY

CIUDAD
DEL
ESTE

ASUNCION

O.D.
ITAIPU

SALTO DO
RIO MONDAY

ACARAY

PTO.
FRANCO

RIO PARANA

FOZ DO
IGUAÇU

CURITIBA

CAMPING

PTO. MEIRA

PUERTO
IGUAZU

BRAZIL

AIRPORT

RIO IGUACU

ARGENTINA

NATIONAL PARK

RIO IGUAÇU

AIRPORT

HOTEL
CATARATAS

POSADAS

HOTEL DAS
CATARATAS

CATARATAS
DO IGUAÇU

N

*The Iguaçu Falls*

every hour). Before returning to town you may wish to turn right, into the beautiful park, and enjoy the thousands of magnificent butterflies. On the Brazilian side, a helicopter ride to the site is available (*Helisul*, tel. 74-2414.)

You will need more time to do the Argentinian side of the falls, but don't spare this time. Buses leave for the falls from Puerto Iguazu (near the Tourist Office in the main street); the trip lasts about half-an-hour. Here, too, you have to pay the admission fee to the park before getting off the bus. Then you can start walking the miles of concrete paths alongside the torrential falls. Walking along these narrow paths is an extraordinary experience, with water thundering by on all sides soaking you with its spray, and the wondrous sight of the falling arc that splits apart at the bottom of the falls. You can walk for hours and not tire of the sublime views, the breathtaking beauty, the unbridled power, the vastness of it all. On this side, the paths lead in various directions, all clearly marked. The last bus back to town leaves at 6pm.

The Argentinian and Brazilian waterfalls are situated on either side of the Iguaçu River ("raging waters" in Guarani — the language of the Paraguayan Indians). In order to travel from one side to the other you must cross the border and the river. Crossing from Argentina to Brazil is a simple matter — all you have to do is walk to the river bank and take the ferry over. (Cars are also allowed on the ferry although not at all seasons). Once in Brazil your passport will be stamped, and then you can board any bus for Foz itself, and go on to the falls.

If you want to cross from Brazil to Argentina, take the bus marked *Porto Meira* from the central bus station to the river, and then the ferry over to Argentina. If you plan to return to your initial side of the border the same day, you don't have to have your passport stamped. Just tell the immigrations official what you're planning — if you're coming from Brazil, you can obtain a visa from the Argentinian consulate in Foz.

When you visit the falls wear comfortable walking shoes with skid-proof soles, and take along a plastic bag in which to put your camera and papers so they won't get wet.

## Itaipú
Twenty kilometers upstream from Foz, at Itaipú, Brazil and Paraguay have erected on the Parana River a giant hydroelectric plant, one of the largest in the world, which since 1984 supplies some 12,000 megawatts of power. This bi-national venture was a heavy economic burden on both countries, and was widely

criticised. The plant was originally intended primarily to meet Brazil's power needs. Paraguay undertook to sell Brazil the surplus energy generated by the dam, and anticipates revenues of hundreds of millions of dollars a year from the sale.

Travel agents in Foz organize trips to the plant, which include slide shows and explanations of the construction of the huge dam. Although you will only be allowed to visit certain sections of the site, the experience is very interesting. The construction of this immense dam caused the destruction of a wonderful nature spot — the Sete Quedas waterfalls, the volume of whose waters was double that of the Niagara Falls. The project caused the flooding of vast areas upstream, and no trace is left of the waterfalls, which are now buried under lago do Itaipu — the lake which was created when the dam was built.

# Minas Gerais

The landscape of Minas Gerais state is mountainous and verdant. The mountain range in the south reaches a height of 2800 m above sea level. The northern sector is mainly rolling hills. Minas Gerais, which has a flourishing cattle industry, is one of Brazil's most fertile states and one of its largest producers of corn, beans, rice, and bananas. However, Minas is most famous for its mines, whence its name (*minas* — mines). The region has large quantities of various natural resources — from iron, gold, manganese, and beryllium to precious stones. Minas is the source of the São Francisco river, which empties into the Atlantic Ocean in Bahia State, north of Salvador.

The discovery of gold in the 18th century put Minas Gerais on the map, and the state still bears the mark of the fevered gold rush that ensued. Many cities and towns were founded then by immigrants from the coast. Mining became an established industry, and Minas' many natural resources were sent abroad through the ports of Santos, Angra dos Reis, Rio, and Vitoria.

## Belo Horizonte
The capital of Minas Gerais, Belo Horizonte, with about 2,400,000 residents, is the third largest city in Brazil. Founded in 1897, it was originally intended to serve as a large and central regional capital. Today Belo Horizonte is endowed with spacious avenues, green squares adorned with statues, and multi-story buildings downtown. The city is an important center for business and industry, and keeps growing at a rapid pace.

Belo Horizonte is not a "tourist town" in the full sense of the word. Although pleasant, cultured, and tranquil, it has few places of interest. On the other hand, there are a number of colonial towns nearby — some of the most famous and beautiful in Brazil — and Belo Horizonte can serve as the starting point for a visit to them.

Area code: 031

### How to get there
**By air:** The Internacional Tancredo Neves airport, 39 km from

the city, was opened at the start of 1984. The terminal is very large and modern, and far exceeds the city's requirements. In fact, the airport handles internal flights only. You can reach the center of town quickly by taxi, or by special buses, which leave throughout the day for the bus terminal downtown. There are also a number of rent-a-car companies at the airport, whose prices vary significantly. If you plan on touring the area, a rented car is certainly the most convenient way to do so — although it is a fairly expensive option.

**By land:** The city's bus terminal, on Praça Rio Branco, serves all the interurban bus lines — those from nearby towns such as Ouro Preto, as well as those from more remote places such as Rio, São Paulo, Salvador, Recife, Vítoria, Brasília, and Campo Grande. The best bus companies operating here are *Penha*, *Itapemirim*, and *Util*. If you want to travel north toward Salvador, via the coast south of Salvador, first head east to Vítoria as many buses continue north from there.

A train runs twice a week between Belo Horizonte and Rio. You can continue by train from Rio to São Paulo.

## Where to stay
*Othon Palace*: Av. Afonso Pena 1050; tel. 273-3844, fax 212-2318. The best hotel in town.
*Savassi*: Rua Sergipe 939, in Savassi (close to the Centro); tel. 212-3266, fax 212-3628. Good value.
*Casa dos Municípios*: Rua Rio Grande do Norte 1017; tel. 226-5177. Comfortable and moderate price, in Savassi district.
*Esplanada*: Av. Santos Dumont 304, Centro; tel. 273-5311. Inexpensive, central location.

## Where to eat
There is a number of good restaurants in the Savassi and Funcionários quarters. Savassi is especially popular among young people and students, and is full of bustling cafes and bars. Funcionarios has many good restaurants, such as the French *Cafe Ideal*, the Italian *La Greppia*, and *La Taverna* which is extremely popular among the young. In the Savassi quarter, we can recommend the *Buona Tavola*, which serves good Italian food, and the *arroz con feijão*, which serves traditional Brazilian fare. One of the best and most popular restaurants in the city is the *Tavares*, at Rua Santa Catarina 64, downtown. The restaurant is not known for its interior decor, but rather for its excellent game and fish.

## Tourist sites

### Downtown

**Praça da Liberdade** is a green square in the city center, which accommodates Belo Horizonte's main attraction — the wonderful **handicraft market**, held every Thursday evening and Sunday morning, where jewellery, leather goods, pottery, paintings, and local foods are sold. The market has a particularly pleasant ambience, and the items on display are unique, very beautiful and attractively priced. You should definitely not miss it. On Saturday afternoons a smaller market is held in the square, where you can find mainly antiques and paintings.

Opposite the square is the **Palacio do Governo**, the Minas Gerais state capitol. The spacious building is stunning, and every evening there is the changing of the guards and the lowering of the flag. Visits must be arranged in advance.

At Rua Bahia 1149, is the beautiful Gothic **Museum of Mineralogy** with a fine collection of minerals and precious stones (open daily, 9am-5:30pm; tel. 238-4203). Nearby is the large **Municipal Park**. The cultural center known as the Palacio das Artes, at the south edge of the park, is used for plays and concerts, various exhibitions, and an expensive and high-quality handicrafts fair.

The **Mangabeiras** quarter, which spreads over the lower slope of the green mountain range south of the city, is the city's most prestigious neighborhood, worth touring for its beautiful buildings and individual character. On the outskirts of the neighborhood, further up on the mountain, is **Mangabeiras Park**, which offers a good view of the city. The park itself has many sporting facilities, and rich and well-tended vegetation. There is an entrance fee.

### Pampulha

Some 10 km from town, in the direction of the airport, is Belo Horizonte's most prestigious suburb, almost a separate city. Pampulha extends around a large artificial lake, surrounded by private homes and impressive estates. This is where the wealthy of the district reside. Close by is Pampulha airport, which, since the opening of the new Tancredo Neves airport, serves only the locals' private planes.

On the southern shore of the lake stands the **Church of São Francisco**, built in 1943. The architect was the well-known Oscar Niemeyer, who designed many of Brasília's buildings. The church is small and not particularly impressive, but is noted for its style, and its beautiful view of the lakeside. East of the Church of São Francisco is the **Mineirão Stadium** — the second largest in the world (after Rio's Maracanã) — built in 1965.

The stadium can hold 130,000 spectators (open to visitors Tues.-Fri., 12.30-6:30pm, weekends 10am-4pm). On the other side of the lake is the **Museu de Arte** (Art Museum), housed in an impressive building surrounded by a lovely garden, also designed by Niemeyer. However, the facade of the museum belies its interior — the collection is poor and unimpressive (Open daily, 8am-6pm, tel. 443-4533).

At the western end of the lake is Belo Horizonte's **Zoologico** (zoo). This spacious and meticulously designed park accommodates over a thousand species of animals in large, pleasant enclosures designed to create the natural environment appropriate to each animal. The zoo grounds abound in greenery, and can be toured by car (open daily, 7am-5pm). Recommended.

## Stalactite Caves

The Belo Horizonte area boasts two stalactite caves, which, although a source of regional pride, are not particularly impressive.

The more beautiful of the two is Gruta do Maquiné, about 125 km from the city, in Cordisburgo. Gruta da Lapinha, 40 km from town, in Lagoa Santa, is less impressive, but nearer. A small museum nearby displays local antiquities, fossils, and stuffed animals.

# The Colonial Towns

The main tourist attractions in the Belo Horizonte area are the picturesque colonial towns spread over the mountain slopes southeast of the city. These towns have preserved their colonial character, with their many churches, unique architecture, and cobblestone streets. Here you can see the work of Brazil's greatest sculptor, Antônio Francisco Lisboa, better known as Aleijadinho. Aleijadinho (1738-1814) suffered from leprosy, as a result of which his body was deformed and his fingers fell off. In spite of this he continued sculpting — indeed his most beautiful and famous works were created after he became handicapped.

**Sabará** is 25 km from Belo Horizonte, and it is the nearest to the capital of all the colonial towns. It has 80,000 residents.

Rua Dom Pedro II preserves much of the architecture of the 18th century. No. 200 of this street is *Solar do Padre Correia*, once a mansion of a wealthy priest, which was built in 1773. The house, which now serves as a town hall, is beautifully preserved, and it has an internal chappel, ornated with gold. At the same street another jam is the **Teatro Municipal**. This theatre was built in 1770 as the town's opera house.

## *OURO   PRETO*

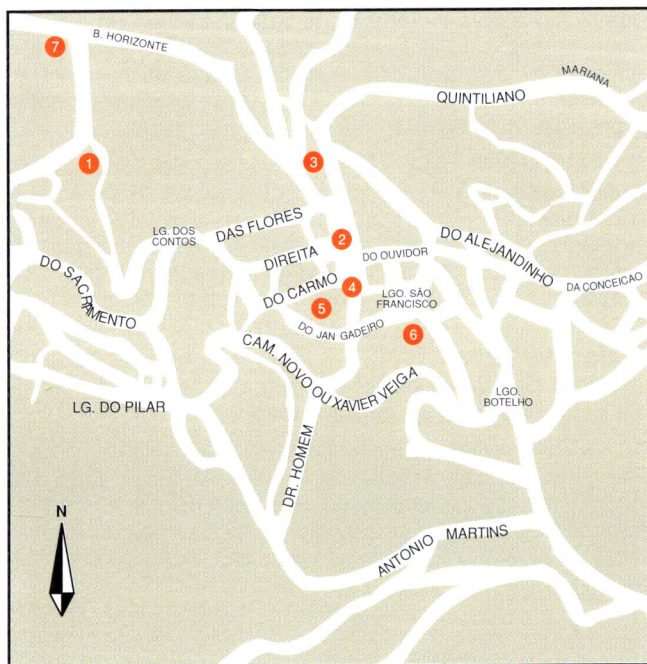

### Index

The town's **Gold Museum** (Museu do Ouro), at Rua da Intendência, is housed in a building erected by the governor of Minas Gerais in 1732. It has a collection of furniture and the tools used by gold miners (open Tues.-Sun. noon-5.30pm). The **Church of Nossa Senhora do Carmo** was built in 1763. Its facade is the creation of Aleijadinho. Other interesting churches are out of town: *Nossa Senhora da Conceição*, about 2 km away, at Praça Getúlio Vargas and *Nossa Senhora do Ó*,

*The charming colonial town of Ouro Preto*

about 10 km away. Both were built in the beginning of the 18th century, and have Chinese influence in the decorations (which are exceptionally rich in the first one).

The tourist information is *Decotur*, at Av. Victor Fantini, tel. 671-1522.

## Congonhas
The town of Congonhas, with its population of 40,000, is a lovely hill-side town in a valley at an elevation of about 900 meters above sea level. It is about an hour bus-ride from Belo Horizonte, and frequent buses link the small town with the capital.

At the top of a hill, the main attraction of Congonhas is the **Basílica do Senhor Bom Jesus de Matosinhos**. Built in 1757 in the baroque style, it offers a nice view of the valley and the town. Here is also the masterpiece of aleijadinho — the statue of the **Twelve Apostles** (open Tues.-Sun. 8am-6pm).

## Ouro Preto
Ouro Preto — "Black Gold" in Portuguese — is one of the most enchanting colonial towns in the world, one of Brazil's tourist gems, and without doubt the crowning glory of a visit to Minas Gerais. It is not suprising that the entire town has been declared

a national monument — an architectural preserve that may not be altered or added to. If you wish to visit only one of the colonial towns, Ouro Preto is undoubtedly the one you should visit.

Ouro Preto was founded in 1698. About 35,000 people live in the town itself, and a similar number in its suburbs. The town is famous for its many churches, each with its own particular charm and grace. Some contain statues by Aleijadinho. The town's streets are narrow, winding, and cobbled. The houses are generally two-story whitewashed buildings with red-tile roofs and wooden verandas — characteristic of the Portuguese-colonial style.

Ouro Preto lies some 1100 m above sea level, and enjoys excellent weather all year round. Green hills surround the town on all sides. The most prominent is Pico do Itacolomi, a huge bluff south of the town that rises to 1753 m above sea level. Don't miss the impressive view from its summit of the surrounding district and especially of the enchanting town at its base.

Many young people come from all over Brazil to study mine engineering at Ouro Preto's famous university. This institution has turned Ouro Preto into a campus town, full of youthful effervescence: every corner has its small bars and clubs, which are packed in the evenings with students.

Area code: 031

## How to get there
Ouro Preto is 98 km from Belo Horizonte over a good road that passes through a mountainous landscape covered in greenery. The small bus terminal handles many daily buses from Belo Horizonte (less than two hours away), as well as direct buses from Rio de Janeiro, São Paulo, and Vitória. The *Util* bus company, which runs most of the bus lines to Ouro Preto, is good and reliable.

## Food and lodging
Ouro Preto has many hotels with varied levels of service and price, and there is usually no problem in getting a room.

*Grande Hotel* de Ouro Preto: Rua Senador Rocha Lagoa 164; tel. 551-1488. Comfortable, spacious.
*Estrada Real*: About 4 km from the town, far off the main road; tel. 273-1144.
*Quinta dos Baroes*: Rua Pandiá Calógeras 474, tel. 551-1056. Only 7 rooms in a splendid old house. Quiet, moderate price, on Morro do Gambá.
*Colonial*: Tr. Camilo Veloso; tel. 551-3133. Moderate, both price and quality.

Young tourists will have no trouble in finding an inexpensive place to spend the night. The town has plenty of student residences, known as *republicas*, whose tenants — students at the local university — are usually quite happy to put up tourists for a paltry sum, and sometimes for free. Make the rounds of the *republicas* until you find one that suits you.

The town has several restaurants. Although conventional restaurants can be found in the large hotels, there are many local gastronomical institutions tucked away on the narrow streets, which are well worth trying.

A good restaurant, serving the traditional fare of Minas Gerais, is the *Casa do Ouvidor*, at Rua Direita 42, tel. 551-2141. Around the main square, Praça Tiradentes, there are a number of snack bars and "fast food" restaurants — which are small and inexpensive. You should definitely stroll through the streets and lanes of the town. At nightfall music can be heard emanating from many places, including discotheques, bars, clubs and restaurants, which makes for a very pleasant stroll.

## What to see

The best way to appreciate Ouro Preto's beauty and charm is simply to wander aimlessly through its small streets. Along the way, visit some of the churches you pass, and experience the youthful atmosphere created by the local students. It is worth visiting the **Church of São Francisco de Paula**, which lies atop a hill at the entrance to the town. From here you have a bird's eye view of the area. The souvenir and handicraft sellers, who congregate outside the church, will try to tempt you with their wares.

Many shops selling tourist souvenirs — especially precious stones and jewellery — are scattered around Praça Tiradentes, which is the center of town. There are also two interesting museums on the square. The **Museu de Mineralogia** (Museum of Minerology) is affiliated with the local university. Although small, it has a wonderful collection of minerals and gemstones. Don't miss it! (Open Mon.-Fri. noon-5pm; weekends 1pm-5pm; tel. 551-1666). The other museum is the **Museu de Inconfidencia**, which was once a prison. Today, the building houses an exhibition of Christian religious art, statues by Aleijadinho, and documents and exhibits that recount the history of Ouro Preto (open Tues.-Sun. 12:30am-5:30pm, tel. 551-1121).

Some 10 km from Ouro Preto, near the town of Mariana, is the goldmine known as **Minas da Passagem**. The chambers and tunnels in this mine, which dates back to the start of the 18th century, stretch to an overall length of 1140 m. The daily output

*In Ouro Preto*

of the mine is now around one kilogram of gold. You can take an organized tour of the quarry, which includes a descent in a miner's cage to an inactive sector of the mine. Later you will see how the gold is extracted from the silt (open daily, 9am-6pm; tel. 557-1255). A bus that leaves Ouro Preto every half hour for Mariana stops at the mine. Recommended.

Not far from the town is an underground waterfall — **Cachoeira das Andorinhas** — hidden inside a cave carved out of the green, rocky landscape. Access to the cave is complicated, since it is visible only after one reaches the edge of a bluff. Be sure to get precise directions before setting out. You can get there by car, or walk from Ouro Preto (about an hour's walk).

The **tourist information** is at Praça Tiradentes 41, tel. 551-2655; another office is at the *rodoviaria*.

## Shopping
The typical handicrafts of Ouro Preto are figures of stone, wood, or clay, jewellery, and of course precious stones, which are plentiful in the area. There are many souvenir shops scattered around the central square. All have a large, fairly similar selection, at a variety of prices. In *Batia*, one of the shops in the square, you will find a large selection of high-

quality and inexpensive articles. At several "strategic points" in town, youngsters will spread cheap souvenirs at your feet. You can usually bargain down the price.

## A boat trip down the São Francisco river

The **Rio São Francisco**, which originates in the mountain range of Minas Gerais, flows north and then east, before emptying into the Atlantic Ocean between Salvador and Maceió, in the north-east. Two steam boats cruise the river on a regular basis, connecting Pirapora in Minas Gerais with the twin towns of Juazeiro and Petrolina, located on opposite sides of the river, the first in Bahia and the second in Pernambuco. The river is navigable for some 1300 km, and a trip all the way down the river by steamboat takes about a week.

The average width of the river is about 500 m, and the surrounding landscape is monotonous and boring. Along its level banks you will see the occasional house and remote town. The boats make short stops at some of these towns — during which you can snatch a hurried tour. The local population is miserably poor, and the illiteracy rate is high. This is the other Brazil, worlds apart from the large cities and the developed south. Here you will discover a simple, primitive world, untouched by the Western pace of life.

There are only two cruises each month. Details and dates of departure can be obtained from the *Companha Navegação do São Francisco* boat company in Pirapora. The company's offices are at 1396 São Francisco Avenue. The company also has offices in Juazeiro, at 3 Coronel Aprigio Duarte street.

# Along the Coast from Rio to Salvador

## Vitória

Vitória, the capital of Espirito Santo state, lies some 500 km north of Rio de Janeiro, and numbers over 250,000 inhabitants. The city lies at the junction of three important routes: north to Bahia, south to Rio, and west to Belo Horizonte and Brasília. Some of the mineral resources of Minas Gerais are exported through the city's harbor. Vitória is situated on an island, and is connected to the mainland by a few bridges. The sandy beaches are suitable for bathing.

The *tourist information* office is *Emcatur*, at Rua de Monjardim 30, tel. 222-0711.

10 Km away from Vitória, on the mainland, is the small colonial town of **Vila Velha**, founded in the 16th century. You can get there on a local bus marked Vila Velha, or on a ferry which leaves downtown every 20 minutes. At the top of the hill are the remains of the monastery of Nossa Senhora da Penha, and a beautiful view of the bay. The beaches of Vila Velha are among the most beautiful in the area, so take along bathing suits.

### Where to stay

*Porto do Sol*: Av. Dante Michelini 3957, tel. 327-2244. At Praia de Camburi, north of Vitoria. The city's best hotel.
*Senac Ilha do Bay*: Rua Bráulio Macedo 417, tel. 325-0111. Good hotel, in a lovely setting, on the tiny island do Bay. Also has a good restaurant.
*Vitória Center*: Av. Jerônimo Monteiro 935, tel. 222-2955.

## Guarapari

The summer resort of Guarapari (55,000 residents) is 54 km south of Vitória. Most of the inhabitants live of tourism. The majority of tourists are Minas Gerais residents who come to spend their vacation by the sea. There is ample accommodation and many places of entertainment along the beach, but they are expensive, and fairly crowded during the summer.

Guarapari offers its visitors peace and quiet. The town has

pleasant beaches and good restaurants, and it has a quiet, agreeable atmosphere.

## Porto Seguro

Porto Seguro, in south Bahia, is one of the oldest towns in Brazil. Little has changed here over the centuries. The small and quiet town has a mere 55,000 inhabitants — the majority make their living from tourism, but some rely on fishing. The beautiful beaches of the vicinity attract many Brazilian vacationers, as well as young travelers from all over the world.

Area code: 073

### How to get there

Porto Seguro is about a 20-hour trip from Rio. Take any of the frequent buses from Rio or Vitória to Salvador. Get off at **Eunápolis**, on the main road. There is a frequent bus service from Eunápolis to Porto Seguro. The trip takes about an hour. The *Sulba* company operates direct buses from Salvador to Porto Seguro (about 10 hours). There is a small airport near the town, improved in recent years in order to develop the tourist industry in the area.

### Where to stay and what to eat

Porto Seguro and the nearby villages have mostly small hotels. Due to local conditions, they are of only moderate standard, or even less, but meet the requirements of most tourists to the area who are usually youngsters and backpackers. The same holds true of the restaurants, most of which specialize in seafood. In Porto Seguro you will have no trouble finding a place at an inexpensive hostel, *pousada*, but most tourists prefer to stay in the nearby villages of Ajuda and Trancoso.

Along the road that leads north of Porto Seguro, to Santa Cruz Cabrália there are a few good tourist-class hotels. Among them:

*Porto Seguro Praia*: 4 Km north of town on the road to Santa Cruz Cabralia, tel. 288-2321, fax 288-2069. The best hotel in the vicinity. All the facilities, including swimming pool and restaurant, in a nice location.
*Portobello Praia*: 7 Km north of town on the same direction, tel. 288-2320, fax 288-2204. Another good hotel in a good location with various facilities.
*Pousada da Gringa*: Close to Porto Seguro, tel. 288-2076. Fine location, basic.

### The beaches

Porto Seguro and its environs are famous mainly for their

beautiful beaches. On your way there, though, you should look around the town itself. There are no places of particular interest, but the town has a tranquil atmosphere, and it is pleasant to wander along the calm streets. There is a tiny fishermen's port here. To the north and south stretch long sandy beaches, which border on coconut palms and thick vegetation.

The small bus terminal is situated near the mouth of the little Rio Buranhém, where there is a small jetty used by the ferries that cross the river. A yacht leaves this jetty daily for a coastal cruise lasting several hours. The yacht anchors en route at several spots, to enable passengers to visit the beaches and go swimming.

### Arraial de Ajuda
Arraial de Ajuda lies some 5 km south of Porto Seguro. To get there you must cross the river by ferry, and then take one of the jeeps or vans, *camionetas*, that leave frequently for Ajuda, or one of the several daily buses that continue to Trancoso.

Ajuda is situated on a hilltop overlooking the coast. During the Brazilian tourist season — the summer vacation — the village is packed with crowds of young people. The pleasant beach at the foot of the hill has many bars, *barzinhos*, some of which also serve fish dishes.

The town itself has plenty of inexpensive hostels (*pousadas*), as well as bars and small restaurants.

### Trancoso
Trancoso, about 12 km south of Ajuda, is smaller than the latter. It has an enchanting beach — a wide, clean stretch of sand, coconut palms and vegetation, and clear, clean water. If you need a break from the vanities of the world, this is the place. Several buses a day from Ajuda to Trancoso follow a road through banana plantations and palm trees. The village itself has a number of small, inexpensive hostels, as well as fish restaurants and bars.

You can reach Trancoso by foot from Ajuda along the coast — a beautiful hike that takes about 4 hours.

# Ilhéus
250 km north of Eunápolis, Ilhéus owes its fame to the world-famous Brazilian author, Jorge Amado. Amado was born here in 1912, and his novels are influenced a lot by the life and atmosphere of the town and its people. Of his many novels the better known ones are *The Violent Land* and *Doña Flor and Her Two Husbands*.

*A beach south of Salvador*

Fans of Jorge Amado would not miss a visit to this old port town, with a population of some 150,000. Yet, you won't find any special attraction here. Stroll along the streets and just get to feel the town and its people.

There are fine beaches close to Ilhéus, well worth an excursion out of town. 20 km south of town along the coast is the small town of **Olivença**, and the road passes many nice beaches and some hotels.

A special resort is *Transamérica Ilha de Comandatuba*, a very expensive deluxe hotel, on an isolated small island beyond Olivença, on the road to Canavieras (tel. 212-1122, fax 212-1114). It is a self contained beach resort with very high standards, and it offers a real tranquility.

In Ilhéus, the **tourist information** is *Ilheustur*, at Praça Castro Alves, tel. 231-1861. Here you will receive information about the town, and about the hotels along the beaches and the cheaper in-town hotels.

## Morro de São Paulo
Morro de São Paulo is a small fishing village, on Ilha de Tinhare, an island near the town of **Valença**. The village itself, whose

houses are scattered on the upper slopes of the hill, lacks distinction, but the beaches below it are among Bahia's most beautiful. Since relatively few tourists come here, the tranquil and isolated character of the place has remained unspoilt.

A ferry leaves Valença daily, arriving at Morro de São Paulo in the afternoon, and returning to Valenca early the following morning (the trip takes about an hour and a half). You can reach Valença on the direct bus from Salvador or from the island of Itaparica (see "Around Salvador"). At Morro de São Paulo it's hard to find anything to eat except for fish, so take along fruit and vegetables from Valença. There are only basic restaurants and hotels, and you can rent rooms from the local inhabitants. Many visitors simply put up tents on the beach.

The splendid tropical landscape is endowed with thick vegetation and palm trees right up to the beach itself. Take a walk along the various hillside paths and along the beaches. If you climb beyond the village, you are sure to encounter small monkeys playing among the trees, and you can enjoy a magnificent view.

## Nordeste: Northeast Brazil

The demography of this region presents some particularly difficult problems. Illiteracy stands at 50 percent, the birth rate is Brazil's highest, as well as the infant mortality rate. Nordeste is home to one-third of Brazil's population, but its contribution to the Gross National Product is only 12 percent. The region's interior hinterland is one of the few places on earth where the feudal system still persists: rich landowners live in large cities, while laborers live on the sugar and cocoa plantations, destitute and totally out of touch with the outside world. Drought is another problem that frequently plagues the region, especially the northern part. Droughts sometimes last several years in succession, followed by a period of especially heavy rains. In 1985, this phenomenon caused disastrous floods, in which many thousands lost their homes.

This notwithstanding, the tourist sees a very different picture: a pastoral scene of usually pleasant towns, small tranquil fishing villages, wonderful beaches that rank among the world's most beautiful, and an almost perpetual summer. The people are simple, friendly and warm. The *jangada*, a raft equipped with a large sail, is very typical of the area and has become one of its symbols.

The large cities of Nordeste are Recife and Salvador. Blacks comprise much of the population here — descendants of slaves brought from Africa, and mulattos of mixed African and Portuguese extraction. The language spoken here is different in accent from that of the south, and so is the music. The samba is less popular; the characteristic dances are the *forro* and the *frevo*, highly rhythmic and extremely fast dances with accordion accompaniment.

The government of Brazil has decided to make the most of the tourist potential of the region and its wonderful beaches, and is investing heavily in developing tourism along the Nordeste coastline. Thus far the coastal area is inhabited mainly by fishermen and by young travelers on vacation, looking to let themselves go in a free atmosphere.

Our route through Northeast Brazil goes along the coast, from Salvador in the south to São Luís in the north, passing by some of Brazils' famous and attractive beaches and resorts.

# NORDESTE

**FORTALEZA**

CEARA

**ATLANTIC OCEAN**

ARACATI

QUIXADA

AREIA BRANCA

MACAU

MOSSORO

RIO JAGUARIBE

ACU

NATAL

RIO GRANDE DO NORTE

CURRAIS NOVOS

CAICO

SAUSA

POMBAL

CAJAZEIRAS

PATOS

CAMPINA GRANDE

SAPE

BAYEUX

CABEDELO

JOAO PESSOA

GOIANA

PARAIBA

ABREU

IGARACU

CARPINA

LIMA

OLINDA

SERRA TALHODA

PESQUEIRA

CARUARU

**RECIFE**

SALGUEIRO

BELO JARDIM

GRAVATA

PERNAMBUCO

ARCOVERDE

CATENDE

PALMARES

BARREIROS

GARANHUNS

PAULO ALFONSO

PALMEIRA DOS INDIOS

SANTANA DO IPANEMA

RIO LARGO

**MACEIO**

ARAPIRACA

SÃO MIGUEL DOS CAMPOS

RIO SÃO FRANCISCO

PROPRIA

PENEDO

BAHIA

**SEREGIPE**

ITABAIANA

LAGARTO

SÃO CRISTOVÃO

RIO REAL

**ATLANTIC OCEAN**

BARRA DE ESNABCIA

SERRINHA

N

FEIRA DE SANTANA

ALAGOINHAS

CACHOEIRA

AMARO

MATA DE SÃO JOAO

CRUZ DAS ALMAS

CANDELAS

**SALVADOR**

TODOS OS SANTOS

Scale

0    50    100    150    200    250 Km

*Bahian gastronomy and atmosphere*

## Salvador-Bahia

Salvador, capital of the state of Bahia, was founded in 1549 and served as Brazil's capital until the mid-18th century. With a population of 2 million people, it is the fifth largest city in Brazil. Blacks predominate here, and many live in grinding poverty. It is thanks to them that the local folklore developed, based on the African culture of the Black slaves. Salvador offers a combination of simplicity, poverty and mysticism, combined with Western sophistication. The well-known Brazilian novelist Jorge Amado excelled in describing this strange world. The city's location on the edge of Baia de Todos os Santos (the Bay of Saints) and its famous beaches, have been an inspiration for writers and musicians. The city's many churches reflect the development of a special kind of Christianity, which combines the beliefs and customs of the Africans with those of the Portuguese.

Salvador weather is about the same most of the year — hot, humid, and rainy. April, however, is the rainiest and stormiest month, and the least suitable time to visit.

Area code: 071

### How to get there

The **2 de Julho Airport**, 28 km out of town, is served by several flights from Brazil's major cities each day, as well as by daily flights from provincial towns. Taxi fare into town is a little steep because of the distance. A special tourist bus goes to Praça da Sé in the center of town. The regular bus follows the same route, and the trip lasts about one hour. In addition, microbuses set out at irregular intervals from the airport for the hotel district at Barra. They stop at the various hotels on request, and are considerably less costly than taxis.

The large bus terminal is quite far from downtown. Two good major bus companies, *Penha* and *Itapemirim*, link Salvador with all the large coastal towns to the north and south. Outside the terminal building there are bus stops for the many bus lines that serve all parts of town. Taxis are plentiful too. The buses are marked with route number and destination; taxis are white or red.

### Tourist services

There are several information bureaus in Salvador. The tourist information bureau at the airport is open whenever the airport is, and has up-to-date information on hotels, restaurants, and tourist sites. The staff is happy to help you make hotel reservations. The main tourist bureau is between Praça Municipal and Praça da

Sé. There are smaller offices at Porto da Barra beach and the bus terminal.

Brazil's major airlines have offices in Salvador, most are downtown. Many countries have consulates here.

## Where to stay
In general, the high-class hotels and the deluxe ones are to be found along the ocean coast of Salvador, some distance from downtown and close to the nice beaches. Barra has many medium class hotels and some inexpensive ones, and it is a good location — it is a better neighborhood of Salvador yet not a long distance from downtown. Cheap *posadas* in downtown and Plourinho attract young travelers.

*Quatro Rodas-Sofitel*: R. Passargada, km 28; tel. 249-9611, fax 249-6946. Out of town, at Itapoã, with nice views and high standards, expensive.
*Bahia Othon Palace*: Av. Presidente Vargas 2456, tel. 247-1044, fax 245-4877. Praia de Ondina, very close to the beach, with nice view to the sea.
*Meridien Bahia*: Rua Fonte do Boi 216, tel. 248-8011, fax 248-8902. Closer to town, on Praia do Rio Vermelho. Good rooms and service, the best in town.
*Enseada das Lejas*: Av. Oceânica 511, Rio Vermelho, tel. 237-1027. Another good and expensive hotel, very small — only 8 rooms. A former private villa on a hill with splendid views of the ocean.
*Marazul*: Av. 7 de Setembro 3937, Barra; tel. and fax 235-2121. Close to Praia do Porto Barra, medium priced.
*Bahia do Sol*: Av. 7 de Setembro 2009, tel. 247-7211. Close to Campo Grande, a short distance from downtown. Medium priced.
*Ondina Praia*: Av. Presidente Vargas 2275; tel. 247-1033. Medium priced, at Praia de Oudina.
*Barra Turismo*: Av. 7 de Setembro 3691; tel. 245-7433. Medium priced, at Porto da Barra.
*Porto da Barra*: Av. 7 de Setembro 3783, tel. 247-4939. At Porto da Barra, inexpensive, with airconditioning.
*Pelourinho*: Rua Alfredo Brito 20; tel. 321-9022. Inexpensive, for young travelers, in the old city.

## Where to eat
Bahia's cuisine is perhaps the most interesting in Brazil. It is highly varied, relying largely on seafood, cooked sometimes in unusual ways, like the *Moqueca* — cooked fish with coconut oil. Enjoy the abundance of tropical fruits, characteristic of the Nordeste. The best place for an informal dinner is the Barra

## *SALVADOR*

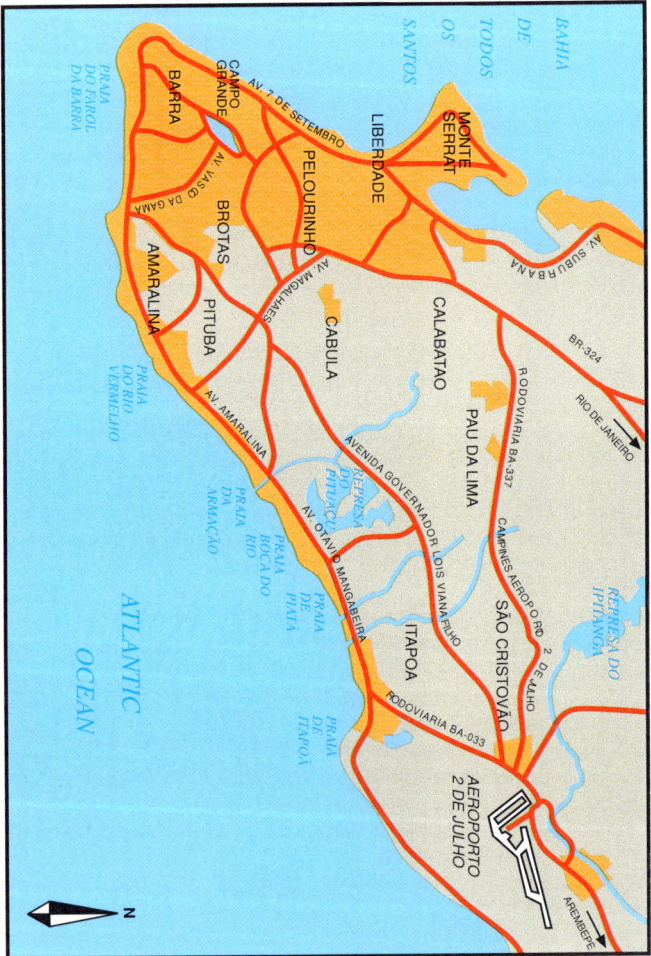

Quarter, which has many bars and restaurants. The Bahia women sell local foods at colorful sidewalk stands. The aromas are appetizing, but conditions are not very hygienic.

*Senac*: Ig. de Pelourinho 13/19; tel. 321-5502. Buffet with many delicacies of Bahia, open for lunch and dinner only. Closed on Sundays.

*The Elevador Lacerda — connecting upper and lower Salvador*

*Iemanja*: Av. Otávio Mangabeira, at Bocca do Rio, tel. 231-5770. Good Bahian food, for lunch and dinner.

*Casa da Gamboa*: Rua Newton Prado 51, Campo Grand, tel. 321-9776. Good traditional food with nice views.

*Casa do Benin*: Praça José de Alencar 29, tel. 243-7629. In Pelourinho, delicious African dishes.

*Mar del Plata*: Praia de Itapoã, tel. 249-4340. Good seafood at Itapoã, lovely beach.

*Frutas do Mar*: Rua Marquês de Leâo 415, Barra, tel. 245-6479. Seafood.

*Bernard*: Rua Gamboa de Cima 11, tel. 321-9402. Good French menu, nice panorama.

## What to see

### Downtown

Central Salvador is divided into two: upper (Cidade Alta) and lower downtown (Cidade Baixa). The two sections are connected by the famous elevator, Elevador Lacerda, built in 1930. At its base is a large square, **Praça Cairu**. Across the way is the large building that accommodates the renowned Salvador market, called **Mercado Modelo**. The building was restored after a serious fire in 1984. Although the market is very touristy, it is lively and colorful. Souvenirs, Brazilian musical instruments, wood crafts, leather goods, lace, and clothing are on sale. Spirited bargaining will bring down the high prices quoted by the vendors. In the square behind the building, *capoeira* dances are sometimes held (see "Folklore"). The market is near a marina where boats depart for the island of Itaparica (see below). Opposite the marina is the round **São Marcelo Castle**, built in the l7th century.

On Praça Tomé de Souza in the Upper City, to the right of the elevator, is **Palacio Rio Branco**, seat of the Governor of Bahia. Here is also the main **tourist office**, *Bahiatursa* (tel. 241-4333), which is open 8am-6pm. Across the way is City Hall. To the left of the elevator, a wide platform overlooks the Lower City and Bahia de Todos os Santos (Bay of All Saints). The street on the left leads to the **Praça da Sé**, a small and neglected square surrounded by small shops. The monument in the center was erected in memory of Fernandez, the first bishop of Brazil (l6th century). This square links up with another, Terreiro de Jesus. Here there are no fewer than three churches. That closest to Praça da Sé is **Catedral Basilica**, one of the most beautiful of the city's 135 churches. Built in 1672, it is an emormous place with gilded interior decorations. In the center of the square a fine *artesania* market is held every day, with Bahian women selling local delicacies from stands.

On the far side of the square is **Igreja São Francisco**, constructed in the l6th century. The exterior facade of this church is not impressive, but the interior is decorated with paintings and gilded decorations (open daily, 10-11am, 2-5pm). To its left is a small church with an impressive Spanish-Baroque facade.

A narrow street, Rua Alfredo Brito, leads away from Terreiro de

Jesus Square. The building on the left was formerly a medical school and today houses the **Museu Afro-Brasileiro** (open Tues.-Sat. 9am-noon; tel. 321-0383). At the end of the street are some small *artesania* shops. Alfredo Brito leads into **Largo Pelourinho**, the neighborhood's central quarter, where the Black slaves once lived. Public floggings, intended as a deterrent to others, took place here. The quarter still retains its colonial atmosphere: the streets are narrow and cobblestoned, and each house is painted in a different color. On this square is the municipal museum and the *Senac* restaurant, a good place to stop and relax, while enjoying the Bahian delicacies.

We follow the street directly opposite. This is Ladeira do Carmo, also called Luiz Vianna. This street ends at another square, **Largo do Carmo**, where you will see a church and the **Forte Santo Antonio**. The fortress played an important role in the Portuguese resistance to the Dutch occupation in the mid-17th century.

Retrace your steps and pass the Church and **Museu do Carmo**. The church has a painted wooden ceiling, and the museum displays religious art, a collection of coins, and an assortment of precious stones. Opposite the museum is a large souvenir store, *Gerson*, selling gems, jewelry, silvercrafts, and Bahian dolls.

### São Joaquim Market
If you wish to get a better and closer idea of Bahia and Salvador life, Feira de São Joaquim is probably the best place. Every day at 6am people from towns and villages around Salvador come here to sell their wares. It is very crowded and dirty, yet authentic, very coulorfull and interesting. Saturday morning is the best time to visit.

The Market is at Av. Jequitaia, about 5 km north of the Mercado Modelo at the Cidade Baixa, along the seafront, in the direction of the peninsula of Monte Serrat.

# SALVADOR — DOWNTOWN

PELOURINHO

PRAÇA DEODORO

R. DA ESPANHA

CAMINO NOVO TABOAO

DOS SANTOS R. DO PACO

R. LUIZ VIANNA FILHO

R. RIBEIRO

R. GOMES

R. SEABRA

AV. ESTADOS UNIDOS

TORQUATO BAHIA

R. DO JULIAO

R. TABOAO

LARGO DO PELOURINHO

RIACHUELO

R. HOLANDA

PRAÇA RIACHUELO

PRAÇA CONDE ARCOS

R. CONDE DEU

R. DA POLONIA

R. SARAIVA

R. BANDEIRA

R. ALFREDO BRITO

R. DE MATOS

R. DA ARGENTINA

R. GONCALVES

R. OUIVRES

R. JOAO DE DEUS

R. GREGORIO

PRAÇA 15 DE NOVEMBRO

PRAÇA ANCHIETA

MIGUEL CALMON

R. DANTAS

R. PINTO MARTINS

R. MONTE

PRAÇA DA INGLATERRA

R. PORTUGAL

R. SÃO JOÃO DUMONT

ALVERNE

PRAÇA DE SÉ

R. DA GAMA

R. TRES DE MAIO

R. FREDERICO REBELO

LADEIRA DA MONTANHA

R. DA GRECIA

R. SANTOS

R. GUEDES

R. DE BRITO

R. ROSARIO

R. DA BELGICA

PRAÇA CAIRÚ

PRAÇA DE SOUZA

R. DA MISERICORDIA

DA FRANCA

R. SALDANHA

R. LADEIRA

R. DE SOUZA

DO TIRA

R. DO TESOURO

R. RUY BARBOSA

R. CHILE

R. VIEIRA

N

*Bahianas at Largo Pelourinho*

*Itapoã beach*

### Monte Serrat

The quiet, peaceful Monte Serrat Quarter is north of downtown, on a peninsula. Buses carrying this name leave the Franca bus terminal in the Lower City. In the center of the neighborhood is the magnificant **Igreja do Bonfim**, built in the mid-18th century. Note the huge altar, frescoes, high painted wooden ceiling, and dark wooden pews. Across from the church is a lovely square planted with date palms.

Next to the church is Rua Plinio de Lima, which we follow for several hundred metres. At its far end is the **Forte de Monte Serrat**, from which there is a nice view of the city of Salvador and of the bay as far as the beaches of Barra. Close by are two churches: Monte Serrat and Boa Viagem.

### The beaches

Of the bay's short, narrow beaches, the most pleasant is **Barra**, which has two 17th-century fortresses, at either end: Santa-Maria and Sao-Diego. Beyond the stately lighthouse is **Farol da Barra** a quieter beach.

The beaches on the Atlantic are better, with long, wide stretches of sand and soaring coconut palms. The most famous beach is also the farthest away: **Itapoã**, the inspiration for many a song. Buses marked *Aeroporto* or *Itapoã* reach this beach after traveling the length of all the other beaches. Two other good beaches along the way are **Jardim de Ala** and **Piatã**. The great Lemanja Festival, in honor of the Kandomela sea-goddess takes place at **Praia do Rio Vermelho** each year (see "Folklore").

## Itaparica

Thirty four islands are found in Todos os Santos Bay, and several are easily accessible by ferry. The most popular with tourists is Itaparica, which is served by a ferry which leaves from São Joaquim Terminal and docks at Bom Despacho. The ferry leaves once an hour from 6am-10pm, and the trip takes about 40 minutes. Buses go from the pier to the towns of Mar Grande and Itaparica. There is also a boat from the port near Mercado Modelo to Vera Cruz on Itaparica; from there the only means of transportation is taxi.

The beaches of Itaparica are beautiful, even though they are not the cleanest. The vegetation is lush and tropical. The houses in the small and very tranquil towns are of simple colonial style. A Club Mediterranee has been established, and many Brazilians and foreigners spend vacations there.

## Feira de Santana

This city of 400,000, about 115 km northwest of Salvador, is the center of a cattle raising district. One of Brazil's finest markets is held here on Mondays, when locals stream to town and peddle their wares, mainly leather products.

A great carnival, the **Micarete**, takes place here about two weeks before Easter, which is very lively and noisy. The streets are packed with dancers and revelers.

There is a frequent bus service between Feira de Santana and Salvador, and the trip takes about 2 hours. The town has several hotels and restaurants, most rather modest.

## The Salvador Carnival

The Carnival in Salvador is unquestionably the wildest and most exciting affair of its kind in Brazil. The festivities continue almost nonstop from beginning to end. Fleets of vehicles called *trios electricos* slowly cruise the city streets, with loudspeakers broadcasting music. Thousands of revelers follow them, dancing and singing for hours on end. The merrymaking dies down for a few hours in the morning, but at noon a parade of dance groups takes to the streets. In the afternoon, the *trios electricos* resume their rounds. This goes on for four solid days. The great dancing processions move mainly through the area between Graça and Praça da Sé, via Praça Campo Grande. The crowd then heads back along parallel streets.

All the nightclubs and discotheques hold special dances for the Carnival, and some of them are really spectacular. The town's elite shows up, and tourists, too, will find this side of the Carnival worth visiting.

Warning: Exuberant and exciting as it is, the Salvador Carnival is also very violent. Muggings and robberies increase during this period, so don't carry any valuables. Try to stay on main streets, and avoid dark alleyways. Keep away from fights, which can develop very quickly.

## Folklore

Bahian folklore is the most rich and interesting in Brazil, thanks to African customs and traditions brought by the slaves. Some of these customs are well integrated into Salvador's daily life. One example is the traditional attire of the Bahian women: beautiful, large white dresses, and special hats. *Figa*, the famous statuette of a clenched fist, is a symbol of luck. *Figas* in various sizes are for sale in every souvenir shop and stall.

In some places in town, including the Mercado Modelo building,

*Capoeira battle dance*

there are street performances of the *capoeira* dance. In this African war dance, two participants kick at each other without making contact. It is fast paced, and the slightest lapse of coordination on the part of either participant is likely to end in injury. The accompanying music is monotonous and simple, played on a drum and a special string instrument called a *berimbão*. Several schools in Salvador teach *capoeira*; visit them and try your skills at this art. One of the best schools is the *Associacão do Capoeira Mestre Bimba*, on Praça Terreiro do Jesus at Rua Francisco Muniz Barreto 1, lst floor (open Mon.-Sat., 7-9pm).

**Candomblé** is a pagan cult originating in Africa. The women handle the rituals while the men deal with secular matters. In the *Candomblé* rite, the women dance for so long and at such a pace that they reach a trance-like state. Visitors may attend these ceremonies. One *candomblé* center is *Terreiro do Oxum Apará*, at Ministro Carlos Coquiejo 44 in Itapoea. Children peddle *Fitinha do Senhor do Bonfim* — a bracelet which, according to *candomblé* tradition, brings luck to its wearer.

The greatest and most famous *candomble* festival is *Iemanjá*, which is held each summer about one month before the

*The Iemanjá Festival*

carnival. Iemanjá is the goddess of the sea, who protects the fishermen and sailors. During this affair, thousands go down to the shore with flowers, incense and other gifts likely to please the goddess. These offerings are handed with great ceremony to the fishermen who they take to sea in their heavily laden vessels. Once they are at a distance from the shore, they toss everything overboard, where Lemanja awaits. This is followed by carnival-like festivities, with dancing in the street until the early morning. The scene recurs all over Brazil, but the one at Praia do Vermelho in Salvador is the biggest and most interesting.

## Maceió

The largest town between Salvador and Recife is Maceió (pop. 550,000) — capital of Alagaos, industrial center of the whole region, and a major port, particularly for the export of sugar and tobacco. Downtown is a noisy place of no interest to the tourist. On the north end of town, along the beautiful Pajuçara beach, there is a green and pleasant promenade with hotels, restaurants and places of entertainment. An *artesania* market takes place here on Sunday evenings.

Area code: 082

## How to get there
The airport of Maceió, about 20 km out of town, is served by daily flights from all major Brazilian cities and Natal, Belem, Manaus, Foz do Iguaçu, and Florianapolis. The *rodoviária* on the outskirts of town is spacious and modern. Several buses leave daily for Salvador, Recife, and other large cities.

Two roads lead from Maceió to Recife. One is the main highway, which crosses the interior. The other is the slow, scenic route, passing through small and picturesque villages, workers in the sugar fields, and along the beautiful coast with its sand dunes and palms.

### Food and lodging
*Jatiúca*: Rua Lagoa da Anta 220; tel. 231-2555, fax 231-9448. The best in town, at Jatiúca beach, a few km to the north.
*Luxor*. Av. Duque de Caxias 2076; tel. 221-9191. Very good, at the promenade.
*Pousada Casa Grande da Praia*: R. Jangadeiros Alangoanos 1528 (Pajuçara), tel. 231-3332. Inexpensive.

Along the promenade you will find various hotels and restaurants.

At Pontal da Barra there are small, simple restaurants serving excellent seafood. One of the best of these is *do Alípio*, at Av. Alípio Barbosa 321 (tel. 221-5186).

## Beaches
The Maceió area has some excellent beaches. About 3 km north of downtown is **Praia Pajuçara** with fishing *jangadas*. At low tide, small natural pools form in the rocks all along the shore. **Praia Jatiúca**, about 10 km north of town, is another fine beach. Beyond it is one of the best beaches in the region, **Praia Graça Torta**, and a little further is **Praia Pratagi**, which also has hidden pools among its rocks.

About 18 km south of town is **Praia Francês**, a broad, beautiful beach with palms. It is deserted on weekdays, but packed with local residents on weekends.

### Pontal da Barra
This little village, about 3 km south of Maceió, is situated on a narrow stretch of sand dunes between the sea and a large lake called Lagoa Mundão. It is bedecked in greenery and palm

trees, and the houses are small and simple. Most people earn a living by fishing or making *artesania*. This is the place to buy lace, which is famous for its beauty and quality.

While visiting, rent a canoe and go out on the beautiful lake. The scenery is particularly gorgeous at twilight.

# Recife

Recife is the capital of Pernambuco, and one of the largest cities in Brazil. Blacks constitute the majority of its population of 1,350,000. The city is situated on Brazil's Atlantic coast and is crossed by several rivers. The meaning of the Portuguese word *recife* is "reef", and the city takes its name from the many reefs along the coast.

Recife was established in 1709, although this is not evident from its modern boulevards, buildings, and the many bridges connecting its various sections. Not far from Recife is the town of Olinda, where the colonial ambience lingers on.

Recife is a major industrial and commercial center, whose development was accelerated by the sugar growing industry.

Area code: 081

## How to get there

For many tourists, Recife is the gateway to Brazil and to South America. Its international airport is about l0 km south of town, near Boa Viagem. Cheap flights are available from most European capitals, Miami, and places throughout Brazil. Taxis are available at the airport. The white taxis charge special fixed rates to take you directly to a hotel. Across the plaza there are regular orange taxis, which charge according to the meter. Buses marked "Aeroporto" leave the terminal every l0 minutes until midnight, traveling via Boa Viagem to the center of town.

Recife's central bus and train stations are situated near downtown. Trains to Maceió and Natal are slow and the bus is better.

## Tourist services

There are tourist information bureaus at the airport, the bus terminal, and the Casa da Cultura de Pernambuco on Rua Floriano Peixoto. All are efficient, and provide information on the whole State of Pernambuco.

Tourists may also make use of a telephone information service.

## RECIFE — DOWNTOWN

### Index

1. Train station
2. Rodoviária
3. Casa da Cultura
4. Palacio do Goberno
5. Palacio da Justica
6. Teatro Santa Isabel
7. Igreja Santo Antonio
8. Mercado São José
9. Igreja de São Pedro

Dial 139 for all relevant information, in English, between 7am-10pm. The Pernambuco Ministry of Tourism, *Empetur*, is at the corner of Avenidà Cruz Cabuga and Rua Artur Coufinho. Many airline offices are on St. Antonio, downtown. Many countries maintain consulates in the city.

## Where to stay

Most of Recife's hotels are concentrated at Boa Viagem, south of town, close to the beach.

*Internacional Othon Palace*: Av. Boa Viagem 3722 (Boa Viagem); tel. 326-7225. Deluxe.
*Savaroni*: Av. Boa Viagem 3772 (Boa Viagem); tel. 325-5077. Less expensive than the former two.
*Casa Grande e Senzala*: Av. Aguiar 5000 (Boa Viagem); tel. 341-0366, fax 341-0120. A pleasant place, a very good restaurant, *Mucama*, serving regional dishes.
*Sofitel Quatro Rodas*: Av. José Augusto Moreira; tel. 431-2955, fax 431-0670. In Olinda. First class, expensive.
*Vela Branca*: Av. Boa Viagem 2494 (Boa Viagem), tel. 325-4470. Basic, small.

The least costly places to stay in Recife are the hotels downtown, especially around the *rodoviaria*.

Recife has many good restaurants. Avenida Boa Viagem is lined with good restaurants and bars, most fairly expensive. The area is crowded at night, and is one of the recommended entertainment spots. The *Lobster* restaurant is at Boa Viagem 2612, and serves excellent seafood. At No. 4780 is the *Rodeio*, renowned for its meat dishes. Order *rodiseio* — all you can eat for a moderate price. *Costa Brava*, Rua Barao Leao 698, excels at local cuisine. For inexpensive eating, try downtown. *Gregorio* is one of the most popular establishments among them. There are also good restaurants, including *Galo d'Ouro* which serves local cuisine and *O Tocheiro*, near the Museu do Homen do Nordeste and just off downtown, which is recommended for its continental cuisine.

Olinda has good restaurants, too. The *Mourisco*, Praça João Alfredo 7, is the best restaurant in town for local offerings. *L'Atelier*, Rua de Melo 9l, is outstanding for its food and service. *Rei da Lagosta*, on the beach at Beira Mar 1255, serves good fish and seafood. There is a Chinese restaurant on the same boulevard: the *Tai-Pei*, very good and relatively inexpensive.

## What to see

As stated, Recife is crossed by several rivers. The commercial and business center is situated on a sort of peninsula called

Santo Antonio. It is a combination of old and new: wide boulevards and skyscrapers alongside narrow alleyways and old houses, crowded markets and ancient churches. At the edge of the peninsula is a broad green square bordered by several important public buildings. To the north is the **Palacio do Goberno**, the seat of government of the State of Pernambuco. Opposite is the **Palacio da Justica**, the courthouse built in a rich neoclassical style. On the west of the square is **Teatro Santa Isabel**, the municipal theater.

On nearby Rua do Imperador, branching off the square, is **Igreja Santo-Antonio** and its abbey. The building's plain facade conceals an opulent interior: an embellished ceiling, an altar of impressive dimensions, and a lovely gilded room to the left of the entrance.

A little further on is a triangular plaza. South of this plaza the streets are narrow, and many are closed to vehicular traffic. The whole area, in fact, is a large and noisy market. Its heart is **Mercado São José**, where typical Nordeste products and handicrafts are sold. The lively and interesting market is open Mon.-Sat. 6am-5pm, Sun. 6am-noon.

There are several churches in the market vicinity. The loveliest is **Igreja São Pedro**, a fine example of Brazilian church architecture. The ceiling is made of wood and adorned with paintings; there are some magnificent altars on the sides, also made of wood and embellished with reliefs. Behind the church is a small abbey, and in front of it is a square surrounded by restaurants and *artesania* shops.

Cross the broad Avenida Dantos Barreto, close to the church of São-Pedro, and continue a few blocks until reaching the **Casa da Cultura**, on the banks of the Rio Capibaribe. The building, erected in the mid-19th century, was the city jail until it became a cultural center in 1975. The prison cells have been converted into *artesania* shops, and folklore performances take place almost every afternoon in the courtyard.

Across the river is the **Boa Vista Quarter**, more modern than Santo Antonio. This district contains bustling commercial areas alongside quiet residential quarters and spacious, green squares.

A short distance from downtown, at Avenida de Agosto 2187, is the **Museu do Homem do Nordeste** — the Anthropological Museum of Northeast Brazil. Here is a tasteful display of Nordeste anthropology: dress, tools, housewares, furniture, and more. The explanations alongside each exhibit are in Portuguese only, but one may request a guided tour in English (open Tues.,

Wed., and Fri. 11am-5pm; Thurs. 8am-5pm, weekends 1-5pm; tel. 268-2000).

**Boa Viagem**, Recife's prestige neighborhood, is south of downtown. It extends along a fine stretch of coast, and has a promenade with luxurious hotels and restaurants. In vacation season, the beach is packed all day long. There is a reef of rocks parallel to the coast which at low tide is exposed, creating little pools of water. On Praça de Boa Viagem, an attractive *artesania* fair is held on weekend afternoons, with music, dancing and refreshments.

## Olinda

About 7 km north from Recife is Olinda. It's a delightful little colonial town, founded in 1536 and stubbornly maintaining its colonial profile. Olinda is famous for cobblestone lanes that wind up the hillside to a lighthouse.

We begin our tour of Olinda at Praça do Carmo, close to the beach. Take the local bus from Avenida Guararapes in Santo-Antonio. The square is named for the old church located there, the **Igreja do Carmo**, built at the end of the l6th century. Although it is not particularly impressive, it is the main church of Olinda. From the square, head up Rua do Bonfim. It is typical of Olinda's streets, lined with one and two-story colonial houses with facades of different colors.

A right turn on the second street off the square, leads uphill to another square with a fine view of Olinda — small houses surrounded by greenery and coconut palms, with church spires protruding here and there. On the right of the square is another church, **Igreja da Sé**, and the square itself is well appointed with bars and *artesania* shops. There is also a small market selling lace, shirts, and wood carvings. Watch the woodcarvers as they work with admirable speed and skill. At night, especially on weekends, the square bustles with young people. They crowd into the bars, some of which play dance music.

Continuing left, we reach the **Museu de Arte Sacra** not far away. The museum is small and not particularly interesting (open Tues.-Fri. 7am-1pm; tel. 429-0036). Farther up the street, where it turns left, is the **Igreja da Misericordia**, which was built in 1540. It affords another beautiful view of Olinda. Follow the street to the foot of the hill, to **Mercado Ribeiro**, with its *artesania* shops. At the end of the street is the **São Bento monastery** with a beautiful church alongside.

## The Olinda Carnival

Olinda has one of the most exciting carnivals in Brazil. It is

*Olinda*

marked with virtually nonstop merrymaking and festivities in the streets; the locals set aside only the morning hours to recharge their batteries for the day and the night ahead. Even then, the more zealous revellers do not stop. Unlike Salvador, where the *trios electricos* lead the dancing parade, Olinda has central platforms where music is played. Music can be clearly heard all along the routes taken by the dancers, as the parades whirl through the streets.

As with every carnival in Brazil, visitors should be wary of violence. Gangs of muggers roam the streets during the carnival period, so stay off dark side streets, leave valuables behind, and do not carry large sums of money.

## Shopping

Recife Shopping Center in Boa Viagem is large and modern. It has shops, boutiques, department stores belonging to large chains, cafes, and restaurants.

The characteristic *artesania* of Recife and Pernambuco are carvings and engravings, lace, and ceramics. Of special interest are ceramic figurines of various characters — lovely but very fragile. The best places to buy them are Praça da Sé in Olinda and Mercado São José. Prices are lower there than at the Casa da Cultura, and the selection is much wider.

## Caruaru Market

Caruaru, about 135 km west of Recife, is noteworthy for its market (open Wed. and Sat. 5am-7pm). It is one of the finest and most interesting in Brazil, and the prices are particularly low. Various local products are sold, especially ceramics, leather and wickerwork. Bus service from Recife is frequent, and the trip takes about two hours.

## Nova Jerusalem

This site is a bad reconstruction of Roman Jerusalem. During Holy Week (*Semana Santa*), an open theater is held here presenting the story of Jesus and his crucifixion. Stages are set up in "Jerusalem", and a different scene is depicted on each as the visitors and actors move from one stage to the next. The drama is interesting even for those who do not speak Portuguese, and the pyrotechnics are impressive. The site is really only worth visiting when there is a performance to see.

The easiest way of reaching Nova Jerusalem from Recife is by organized tour, which takes you to and from the performance in a comfortable bus. The second possibility is less expensive: take a bus from Recife to Caruaru and change for Fazenda Nova, which is within walking distance of Nova Jerusalem. If there is no bus back to Caruaru at the end of the show, hitch a ride in one of the jeeps leaving Fazenda Nova.

## Gaibu

One of the most beautiful beaches in the Recife area is Calheta, within walking distance of the village of Gaibu. The beautiful beach borders a small, deep bay with clear blue water, and its narrow strip of sand is edged with hills and greenery. The village is lively and many young people come here on holiday to enjoy the beautiful beaches. Gaibu is reached from the town of Cabo, not far from Recife.

## João Pessoa

Some 120 km north of Recife on the shores of the Rio Paraíbam, is João Pessoa (pop. 440,000), capital of the State of Paraíba. It is a grey industrial town, with nothing of interest to tourists apart from the impressive, 18th-century **Igreja São Francisco**.

About 7km away is the beautiful beach and fishing village of **Tambau**, with a very expensive hotel and a good restaurant. Approximately 11 km to the south is Cabo Branco, the easternmost point in the Americas. The view is beautiful, and there is a good restaurant.

The airport is about 11 km from downtown, and planes land every day from all over Brazil. The bus terminal is a little far out from downtown. It is served by several buses every hour from Recife, and others from Natal and Fortaleza.

Area code: 083

## Natal

Natal (pop. 580,000) is the capital of Rio Grande do Norte. The city, located on the eastern bank of the Rio Potengi, is the region's industrial and commercial center. While it does have several interesting sites, the real attraction here is the proximity of some marvelous beaches.

Area code: 084

### How to get there

The airport is about l5 km out of town, and is served by flights from all major Brazilian cities. The bus terminal is at Cidade da Esperança, quite far from downtown. Traveling time to Recife is about five hours, to Fortaleza about seven hours.

### Where to stay

*Natal Othon*: Av. Cafe Filho 822; tel. 222-2055.
*Sambura*: Rua Prof. Zuza 263; tel. 261-0611. Moderate.
*Casa de Mãe*: Rua Pedro Afonso 153; tel. 222-9920. Serves excellent local cuisine at reasonable prices.
*Do Marinho*: Rua Areial 267; tel. 222-1471, in the downtown area, very good and reasonably priced.

*Xique-Xique*: Avenida Afonso Pena 444; tel. 222-4426. An elegant restaurant.
*Carre Assado do Lira*: Rua Mipibu 657, tel. 222-9937. Very good regional dishes.

## What to see

Stop at the municipal tourist bureau at Avenida Hermes da Fonseca 970 for information on the various sites and how to reach them. The main street in town is Avenida Rio Branco. At the central square, **Praça João Maria**, there are two churches: one old and traditional, the other modern. Natal's oldest structure (16th century) is **Forte dos Reis Magos** — the bastion on the Praia do Forte. **Mercado do Alecrim** is an *artesania* market which is worth visiting.

About 20 kilometers from Natal is a missile installation known as the *Barreira do Inferno* (Devil's Barrier). One can visit here, but only in organized groups. Make reservations 48 hours in advance at one of the travel agencies that organize these outings.

### Beaches

There are several marvelous beaches in the immediate vicinity of Natal. One of the most beautiful is **Genipabu**, about 30 kilometers north of town. There is a large sand dune, with many palms, which slopes steeply into the blue sea. Another excellent beach is **Ponta Negra**, 14 kilometers south of town, and farther away is another beautiful beach, **Piranji**.

# Fortaleza

Fortaleza (pop. 1,700,000) is the capital of the State of Ceará. It is a pleasant city which enjoys the natural amenities of Nordeste: almost year-round summer, lovely beaches, and friendly people. The *artesania* in this city is famous throughout Brazil for its beauty and quality. The superb lobster delicacies are also outstanding.

Area code: 085

### Transportation

The Fortaleza airport, about 9 km from town, is reached by daily flights from almost all the large cities of Brazil, as well as Manaus, Natal, Florianopolis, and Foz do Iguaçu. The airport is not noted for its services. The passenger terminal is old and has no air-conditioning, and the tourist office is inefficient. The special airport taxis are white, and the regular ones are orange.

**Means of transportation in the Nordeste**

*Sunset in Fortaleza*

The spacious, efficient bus terminal is outside the city center. Several buses arrive every day from Recife after a 13-hour trip. The bus ride to Belem takes about 24 hours, as does the trip to Brazilia.

From the bus terminal, bus 502 heads for downtown, reaching Praça José de Alencar, the municipal central bus station.

### Food and lodging
*Esplanada*: Av. Kennedy 2000; tel. 244-8555. Deluxe. All rooms with balconies facing the sea.
*Imperial Othon Palace*: Av. Kennedy 2500; tel. 244-9177. Deluxe.

*Praia Centro*: Av. Tabosa 740, tel. and fax 211-1122. High standards with moderate prices, at the downtown.
*Beina Mar*: Av. Kennedy 3130, tel. 244-9444. Moderate price, good location at the sea-front.
*Praia Mar*: Av. Kennedy 3190, tel. 244-9455. The same fine location as the latter hotel, less expensive.

*Trapiche* is an excellent fish restaurant with unsurpassed and renowned lobster delicacies. It is situated at the far end of Avenida Kennedy at No. 3956. Another restaurant which serves very good seafood is the adjacent *Aquarius*. *Sandra's*, on Praia do Futuro, is one of the best restaurants in town. *Mikado*, next to the Museum of History, serves good steak.

**What to see**
Downtown bustles during the day, and traffic inches along. At Avenida Pompeu 350 is the **Centro de Turismo**, built in the mid-19th century as the city jail. Today it houses an *artesania* market, a restaurant, and a tourist office (on the first floor). The second floor accommodates **Museu de Arte e Cultura Populares** (open Mon.-Fri. 7am-6pm, Sat. 8am-noon). The museum has a large model of a *jangada*, the typical raft of Nordeste fishermen, and displays various artifacts of daily life.

Not far from the tourist center is a large fortress, **Fortaleza Nossa Senhora da Assunção**, which lent the city its name. It was built by the Dutch, and renovated in 1810. On Praça da Sé is the large, strange **Catedral da Sé**, which from the outside looks like a fortress. In the center of the square stands a statue of Emperor Dom Pedro II. The covered city market is next to the square. The *artesania* here is fantastic; don't hesitate to haggle.

The wealthy section of Fortaleza is in the east. Three beaches — Meireles, Iracema, and Mucuripe — are really one stretch of shore, with Avenida Kennedy and its lovely promenade alongside. Most of the town's prestigious hotels and restaurants are found here. Every evening between 6-8:30pm a pleasant, well-stocked *artesania* market opens along the promenade, and everyday around 3pm the *jangada* return to the beach at the end of Avenida Kennedy. One can watch the fishermen bring in their catch, and buy some fresh fish at the same time.

The **Museum of History and Anthropology** is at Avenida Barão de Studart 410, but it does not have very interesting exhibits. Across the way is the modern government building; next to it is the mausoleum of Castelo Branco, and his wife. He was a president of Brazil, who died in an aviation accident.

**Shopping**
Fortaleza offers a wide variety of interesting and beautiful *artesania*, at some of the lowest prices in Brazil. The hammocks for sale here are renowned for beauty, quality, and low price. Bottles of multicolored sand, superb embroidery, and marvelous ceramics are typical local *artesania*.

At Central de Artesanato, Avenida Santos Dumont 1500, one can watch the artists at work. If you are buying, bargain over the prices. Another good place to buy *artesania* is Mercado Central. Several shops sell hammocks along the streets just west of Praça da Sé. Prices are low, the selection is large, and quality is good. Dozens of fine shops on Avenida Monsenhor Tabosa stock *artesania*. They are open Mon.-Sat. 8am-4:30pm.

## The Beaches of Ceará

The State of Ceará has about 600 kilometers of beaches, and they are undoubtedly Brazil's loveliest: golden sand, white dunes, palms, and kilometer after kilometer free of human presence. Several beaches attract throngs of young people from Brazil and elsewhere. The most famous and popular is **Canoa Quebrada**, just outside the city of **Aracati**. Buses reach Aracati from Natal and Fortaleza, and Aracati itself is a point of departure for vehicles heading for Canoa Quebrada. This village bustles with life and offers an abundance of bars and simple little restaurants.

Closer to Fortaleza, 78 km to the southeast, is the lovely **Morro Branco** beach with its multicoloured sand. If you prefer an excellent beach in Fortaleza's immediate vicinity, **Praia do Futuro** is the place you should go to.

The village of **Paracuru** is a three-hour bus ride west of Fortaleza. The entire coastal area here consists of splendid dunes, which descend steeply into the ocean. After heavy rains, fresh water gathers in pits carved into the dunes. On weekends the place is packed with young people from Fortaleza. The surfers who spring into action when the sea picks up are well worth watching. Weekend *forro* parties at the oceanside bar attract crowds of young people from Fortaleza and the vicinity.

**Jericoacoara**, a remote and tiny village, is "discovered" by travelers only in recent years. Most of its 500 families leave on fishing, and only a few of them run the several *pousadas* and restaurants. All unspoilt dunes, the highest of which is 100 m, are in the same direction as a result of the strong wing coming from the ocean. The place enjoys exceptional beauty and tranquility. Near the village there are a few small caves close to the sea. A nice walk of a few kilometers is along the coast to Preá, another small village to the east of Jericoacoara.

Jericoacoara is some 300 km west from Fortaleza. It can be reach by bus to Bela Cruz (6 hours), and then a short drive to the village.

## São Luís

São Luís, founded by the French in 1612, is between Fortaleza and Belem. This city, the capital of Maranhão, is situated between two bays on an island linked to the mainland by a

*Cleaning the fish for dinner*

bridge. Although its downtown area is bustling, a 17th-century ambience lingers on. The colonial architecture is lovely, but most of the buildings are rundown. On the northern side of the channel is the São Francisco neighborhood, the "New City" of São Luís, with well kept residences. São Luís is known for the great extremes of its tides. In the afternoon, at low tide, vast areas of the sea bed become visible.

Area code: 098

## How to get there

The airport of São Luís, which is small but efficient, is situated about 10 km out of town, and has many connections every day from all parts of Brazil. Taxis wait at the airport's exit, and buses set out for town every hour. The São Luís bus terminal is about 5 km from downtown. The trip from here to Fortaleza takes about 16 hours, and there are direct buses to Recife as well. The trip from here to Belem is very difficult, and parts of the road are unpaved. Two buses cover the route every day, and the trip takes about 13 hours.

## Where to stay

*Sofitel Quatro Rodas São Luís*: Av. Aviscencia s/n; tel. 227-0244, fax 227-4737. Out of town, excellent; lovely landscape.

*Jericoacoara*

*Vila Rica*: Av. Dom Pedro II 299; tel. 232-3535, fax 222-1251. Centrally located.
*Lord*: Rua Nazaré 258; tel. 222-5544. Inexpensive.
*Central*: Av. Dom Pedro II 258; tel. 232-3855. Inexpensive, at the Centro.

## What to see

The historical center of São Luís is along Avenida Dom Pedro II. On this lovely boulevard stands the government palace, **Palacio dos Leoes** (Palace of Lions), built in 1776 (open Tues., Wed. and Fri., 3-6pm, tel. 222-0355). Continue up the avenue to the place where it turns into **Praça Dom Pedro**. On this square is **Palacio Arquiepiscopal**, the bishop's residence, and next door is **Catedral da Sé**. Built in 1763, it is one of the most beautiful churches in town. Dom Pedro is linked to another square — Praça Benedito Leite, where there are several little bars as well as some shops and hotels. The cobblestone streets around this square are very old and most of the houses date from the 18th and 19th centuries.

From here, turn onto Rua do Sol and follow the street to a three-sided piazza, **Praça João Lisboã**. Another two blocks and we reach Teatro Artur Azevedo, constructed in 1817. A little further is the **Museu Historico e Artistico do Maranhão**, (open

Tues.-Fri. 2-6:30pm, weekends 3-6pm). Further along the road is another square, **Praça do Panteon**, where the municipal library stands. Next to this square is **Quinta do Barão**, which is a good example of the colonial estates of Nordeste.

Again, don't miss the tides. Go down to the beach at Avenida Beira Mar early in the morning, when high tide is at its peak, and come back in the afternoon to see how far the ocean has receded.

A local festival, **Bumba Meu Boi**, is held here in the second half of June. Its official date is June 24, but the festivities begin several days earlier. Watch dance parades in the streets and note the traditional costumes.

## Alcântara

Alcântara is opposite São Luís on the western side of São Marcos Bay. It's an interesting small town, which served in the distant past as the capital of Maranhão. All that remains of its golden years in the 17th and 18th centuries are ruins, a few miserable streets, dilapidated colonial houses, and a handful of rundown churches. The ruins of **Casa do Imperador** are overgrown with vegetation, as are the remains of **Forte de São-Sebastiao** (mid-17th century). The **Museum of Alcântara** is open daily 9am-2pm.

A week of traditional local festivities begins on May 15. A "prince" and "princess" for the week are elected each year, and a carnival atmosphere prevails.

Boats from São Luís set out for Alcântara every morning at 8am from the marina at Praça Pinto Martinez, opposite Avenida Dom Pedro II. The trip takes about an hour and a half. The boat returns to São Luís between 1-2pm, depending on how low the tides are that day. Once you arrive, find out the time of the return trip. Alcântara itself has a couple of little hostels and a few simple seafood restaurants.

# The Amazon Basin

The Amazon River and the jungle covering the immense Amazon basin fire the imagination as few other sites can. The river's tremendous dimensions are beyond human conception, and the endless jungle, with its innumerable species of animals — for whom this is the last stronghold — is one of nature's most incredible wonders.

The Amazon, the world's second longest river, originates in the Andes of western South America and spills into the Atlantic Ocean after a journey of 6280 km. Its volume is the world's largest by far — 15 times that of the Mississippi. In certain areas it is tens of kilometers wide. Hundreds of tributaries drain into the huge Amazon basin. Many of the tributary rivers which feed into the Amazon and flow through Brazil have their origins in Bolivia, Peru, Equador, Colombia and Venezuela.

Brazil began developing the Amazon region, which comprises a major portion of its territory, in the 1950's. This development included the large-scale project of building the Trans-Amazon Highway. The project was a failure, and it was severely detrimental to the environment and to the tribal Indian population. Once the road was finished, it proved passable by motor vehicle during the dry season only, and the fortune taken from Brazil's impoverished national coffers had gone down the drain.

The route through the Amazon goes from Belém to Manaus, and from there splits into three possible directions: north — to Boa Vista and on to Venezuela; west — to Benjamin Constant, Liticia and on to Colombia or Peru; and south — to Porto Velho. From Porto Velho it is not far to Bolivia, and it is possible to go to the mid-west to Cuiaba.

We describe all these possibilities, but the main route on our trip is that which goes to Porto Velho and the mid-west.

## Belém

Belém is situated on the southern bank of the Amazon delta. This city, capital of the state of Pará, has a population of about 1,200,000. Until the 1960's, when a road was built from Belém

## *THE AMAZON BASIN*

*On the boat from Belém to Manaus*

to Brasília country's interior, the city was accessible only via river and air routes. Founded in 1616, Belém today serves as a commercial and industrial center, mainly for wood and textiles. Its port is the largest and most important on the Amazon.

Situated slightly south of the equator, Belém has a tropical climate — very warm and muggy. All year round at the stroke of 3pm, they say, heavy downpours wash the city, and certainly during our brief stay there, that's exactly what happened.

Area code: 091

## How to get there
Belém's international airport serves regular flights from all over Brazil, daily flights from Buenos Aires, and weekly flights from Miami and Spain.

Belém can be a point of departure or final destination for a cruise on the Amazon. Most passenger boats sail to Santarém and Manaus, with occasional voyages to Porto Velho. The journey upriver to Manaus takes about 5 days, and the ships are packed with passengers. The river is very wide in this area, so don't expect to see breathtaking tropical jungle scenes from the middle of the river. There are three passenger classes:

cabins (the most expensive), first class (on deck in the fresh air), and second class, in the ship's interior (hot, crowded, and noisy because of the engine). Never mind the low price; pass up second class! You would have to come equipped with hammocks, mosquito netting, and bug-repellent. All tickets include meals, but they are far from filling; it is a good idea to bring fruit. Cruises are organized by the government-owned *Enasa* company, and the ships set sail from Porto de Enasa on Avenida Castilhos Franca.

The local bus terminal is located 5 km from the center of town. A few buses leave daily for Brazilia. There is a bus to Santarém once a week, which travels along the Trans-Amazon Highway. Service is more frequent to Marabá, from which Santarém is easily accessible. Two buses a day depart for São Luís, traversing a difficult road, and two others go to Fortaleza and Recife. There is a direct bus every day to Rio de Janeiro.

The flight from Belém to Manaus deserves special mention because of the gorgeous scenery it flies over. The flight crosses the Amazon where it is at its widest — so that one sees one bank only, the other is hidden somewhere beyond the horizon!

## Food and lodging
*Hilton*: Av. Pres. Vargas 882, tel. 223-6500, fax 226-8761. Excellent; centrally located.
*Novotel*: Av. B. Sayão 4804; tel. 229-8011, fax 229-8709. Far from downtown, but runs a frequent shuttle service.
*Vanja*: Tr. Benjamin Constant 1164; tel. 222-6688. Moderate.
*Novo Avenida*: Av. Pres. Vargas 404; tel. 223-8893.

Near the Castello fortress is a good fish restaurant, *Circulo Militar*. Its specialty is a typical Belém fish dish called *pirarucu*. *O Outro*, at Avenida José Malcher 982, serves good local cuisine. *Hotel Equatorial*, downtown at Avenida Braz de Aguiar 612, has two good restaurants: the continental *1900*, and the *Terrace Grill*, which specializes in meat dishes.

## Tourist services
The municipal tourist office is at Avenida Nazaré 231. Several countries, including the United States, Great Britain, Venezuela, and Colombia, have consulates in the city.

International phone calls can be made at the bus terminal and the airport. An additional phone exchange is located downtown at Praça da Republica, at the corner of Vargas and Riachuelo. The phone company is called *Telepara*.

A recommended travel agency is *Ciatur*, with offices at Avenida Presidente Varga 645.

## What to see

Belém's commercial center is situated at **Praça da Republica**, a spacious and green square. In the center of the square stands the splendid **Teatro da Paz**, built in 1874 in neoclassical style. Worth a visit (open Mon.-Fri, 8am-noon and 2-6pm; tel. 224-7355).

Close to the river's edge is the triangular Praça Castilhos França, the heart of the city's old district. A little beyond it is the harbor for fishing boats and a colorful, crowded market — **Mercado Ver o Peso**. We continue along the riverside until reaching **Forte do Castelo**, a bastion probably dating from the nineteenth century, close to the landing place of the city's Portuguese founders. Across the way, still at the square, is Belém's oldest church built in the early 17th century.

Across town on Avenida Nazaré is the enchanting **Basilica da Nazaré**, its interior lined with gilded ornamentation and frescoes. Somewhat further, at Avenida Magelhães Barata 518, is **Museu Emilio Goeldi** (open Tues.-Thurs. and Sat., 9am-noon, 2-5pm; Fri., 9am-noon, Sun., 9am-noon; tel. 224-9233). This large museum encompasses a zoo and a botanical garden, which exhibit a selection of jungle flora and fauna. There is also an interesting anthropological museum.

## Ilha do Marajó

From Belém, this island is reached by a 5-hour river cruise or a 30-minute flight in a light plane. Large areas of this enormous island (50,000 km$^2$) are almost uninhabited; its population of 250,000 is concentrated in 7 different towns, the main one being **Soure**. Marajó island is unique for its many buffalo herds. There are a number of farms (*fazendas*) on the island where tourists can stay, and from which one can set out on wildlife observation safaris.

Several travel agencies in Belém organize excursions to the island, which set out from the city itself. They are good, and recommended, but expensive.

There are 3 *Fazendas* which have offices in Belém, to which you can call and get information and make reservations:

*Fazenda Bom Jardim*: tel. 224-3233, 223-3177.
*Fazenda Jilua*: tel. 225-0432.
*Fazenda São Marçal*: tel. 223-4099, 223-3177.

## Mosqueiro

The town of Mosqueiro is located on an island of the same

*Santarém*

name. It is reached by an excellent road from Belém 86 km away, and a bridge connects the island with the mainland.

The island is covered in tropical jungle, and the beaches are sandy and pretty — especially **Baia do Sol**, 26 km north of town. There are other lovely beaches west of the town. In Mosqueiro there are several hotels and restaurants.

## Santarém

Halfway between Belém and·Manaus, on the Amazon's south bank near its confluence with the Tapajos, is the city of Santarém (pop. 240,000) which serves as a center of the lumber and textile industries. The convergence of the two rivers is an impressive sight, as the rivers maintain their different colors even after they merge. Passenger boats set out from Santarém for the confluence. Beautiful, sandy beaches are close at hand. Worthy of special mention are those along the Tapajos. In the rainy season, however, the river submerges every strip of beach.

It's about a two-day boat trip from Belém or Manaus to Santarém, and flights between Belém and Manaus stop over in Santarém. Most of the hotels and restaurants here are, at best, mediocre.

*The glorious Teatro Amazonas*

## Manaus

Manaus is on the Amazon's northern bank, about 1700 km upriver. With a population of about a million, it is the largest of the river cities. Manaus is the capital of Amazonas, Brazil's largest state. Until just a few years ago, there was no land access to Manaus; the city could only be reached by air or river. It has a large harbor, and because the river is so wide and deep, even large ships can sail as far as Manaus.

Today there are roads to Manaus from Porto Velho in the south and Boa Vista in the north. Just a few kilometers out of town is the confluence of the Amazon's two largest tributaries: the Rio Negro and the Rio Solimões. Manaus itself lies on the bank of the Rio Negro ("Black River"), aptly named for its black water.

At the end of the last century, Manaus became a boom town after rubber was discovered nearby. The Amazon area was the world's only source of this commodity at the time, and rubber accounted for 25% of Brazil's exports in 1880. The famous opera house, built at the time, mirrors that prosperity. As suddenly as prosperity came, however, so did it end. Malaysia also began growing rubber trees, and Manaus lost its monopoly and its mad attraction for investors. Today it is a city like any other

— busy, crowded, and dull — and the opera house stands like a monument to the days of glory. In 1967, in an attempt to revive Manaus' economy, the city was declared a duty-free zone. This turned it into a bustling shopping center. Tourists arriving in Manaus are asked to declare all valuables in their possession upon arrival, and all purchases upon departure.

Area code: 092

## How to get there
**Eduardo Gomes International Airport**, about 14 km from downtown, is modern and spacious. Connections to and from the airport are handled by fixed-rate taxis and by buses that run every 30 minutes. There are many flights between here and destinations throughout Brazil, and there are other regular connecting flights with most South American capitals, Mexico City, and Miami.

The harbor where the passenger boats dock is close to downtown and hums with people and activity. Schedules are irregular. There are frequent trips between Belém (5-day journey) and other vessels travel between Benjamin Constant or Tabatinga, both situated where the borders of Brazil, Peru, and Colombia converge (about 8 days journey). There is an occasional direct boat service between Leticia on the Colombian border, and Iquitos in Peru. Boats traveling between Porto Velho and Manaus leave more frequently.

Even today, despite the Trans-Amazon Highway and the clearing of a road to Porto Velho, most traffic is still handled by river and air transport. The bus terminal, *rodoviária*, is located out of town, on the way to the airport. It is reached from downtown by buses marked "Aeroporto" or "Praça 14". From the terminal, buses leave several times a day for Porto Velho, and there is a daily bus to Boa Vista, en route to Venezuela. Buy tickets several days in advance, because the buses are usually full.

## Where to stay
*Tropical Manaus*: tel. 238-5757, fax 238-5221. The best in town, and the most expensive.
*Amazonas*: Praça Adalberto Vale, tel. 534-7979/7879, fax 234-7662. Located downtown.
*Internacional*: R. Dr. Moreira 168; tel. 234-1314. Moderate.
*Nacional*: R. Dr. Moreira 59; tel. 233-0537. Inexpensive.

## Tourist services
The spacious airport has an efficient tourist information office. Call direct from there to the city's major hotels. Additional tourist

offices are located downtown at Praça 24 de Otubro, at the floating harbor, and in the main Post Office at Marechal Deodoro 117. Several travel agencies in town organize jungle tours. Selvatur (offices on Praca Adalberto Vale, in the *Amazonas* hotel) is recommended.

Most South American countries, and some European countries, station diplomatic representations in Manaus. The United States Consulate is at Rua Maceió 62.

## What to see

The first stop and most famous site in Manaus is the fabulous opera house, **Teatro Amazonas**. This magnificent building, built in 1896 and renovated in 1974 and in 1990, reflects the affluence and prosperity of that earlier period. Its facade is decorated with columns and statues, and crowned with a gilded dome. The interior is divided into several halls. The largest is the playhouse, with seating for 700. The ceiling is adorned with four paintings, each depicting a different type of art: music, dance, drama, and opera. Worthy of particular attention is the ballroom, which is the loveliest hall of all. Note the floor, made of 12,000 wooden strips. The walls are covered with paintings depicting Amazon jungle scenes, and the ceiling is also decorated. The marble was imported from Italy. The opera house, open Tues.-Sun. 9am-6pm, is situated on Praça São Sebastião. There is a beautiful fountain in the square — a monument to navigation. On the right is the **Igreja São Sebastiao{** (São Sebastião Church). Not far from the square is the neoclassical **Palácio da Justiça** (courthouse).

The tax-free shopping district lines the narrow, crowded downtown streets. Along the river is the **Porto Flutuante**, the floating harbor. Owing to major fluctuations in the river's water level, the piers are not fixed but are left to float. River boats drop anchor here, and there is a continuous bustle of loading and unloading. Close to the harbor is the crowded **Mercado Municipal** (municipal market), with the fishing boat jetty across the way. If you want to explore the Amazon on your own, find a guide here, and remember to haggle over the price.

**Museu do Indio** (the Indian Museum) is at the corner of Avenidas 7 de Setembro and Duque de Caxias. The museum depicts the life of Rio Negro's Indian tribes — clothing, handicrafts, and ritual implements (open Mon.-Sat. 8-11am and 2-5pm.)

**Palacio Rio Negro** at Avenida 7 de Setembro currently serves as the governor's residence. Formerly it was the splendid home of a rich German merchant.

*The lively floating port at Manaus*

## Jungle excursions

Manaus is a good point of departure for tours of the Amazon and the jungle. The river is immensely wide in this area, with a proliferation of islands, narrow channels, and lovely lagoons. Remember, however, that this is a settled area, and do not expect a voyage into the unknown, or fascinating encounters with wildlife. Only an expensive trek lasting many days can provide such an adventure.

There are two ways to explore the jungle. The first is to join a travel agency's organized tour, and the other is to hire a guide with a canoe, and negotiate with him the duration, route, and price of the trip (which would be much lower than the organized tour). The guides can be found in the marketplace and the adjacent fishermen's jetty. Always bargain, and never pay more than half the sum in advance! In any event, these excursions are very expensive — generally more expensive than tours elsewhere along the Amazon.

Most tours probe little channels bursting with tropical vegetation. One may also fish for piranhas, and trap crocodiles. Here one can see the huge water plant called *Vitoria Regia* which grows up to 3 meters in diameter. There are also rubber trees and, if you are fortunate, you may see some wildlife. An impressive

*The Vitoria Regia plant*

sigt is the confluence of the Rio Negro and Rio Solimões. The waters of the Rio Negro really are black, and the waters of Rio Solimões are grey. There is no doubt about where the convergence occurs. If you set out with a guide, make sure to include this in the itinerary.

It requires several days' travel to penetrate deep into the jungle. We recommend spending only two or three days there. After this the sites become routine, and an additional few days of trekking will not produce anything really new.

## Shopping
The tax-free shopping center, as mentioned, is downtown between Rua 7 de Setembro and the river. Dozens of shops offer imports from clothing to photo and electronics equipment. Prices are low by South American standards, but tourists from the United States and most European countries will not find bargains. There is a legal limit as to how much one can buy.

Typical *artesania* of this region include Indian art, woodcraft, and ceramics.

# Boa Vista
Boa Vista (pop. 75,000), capital of the Roraima area, is 800 km north of Manaus in the middle of a vast, monotonous savannah. Two roads continue from there: one to Santa Elena on the Venezuelan border 200 km to the north, and the other to Normandia on the border with Guyana, 140 km away.

Daily flights arrive from Manaus, and a few flights a week touch down from other cities. The airport is only 4 km away. There is also a daily bus from Manaus (about 20 hours).

The city has a few hotels; most are basic in price and services. The same holds true for the restaurants. The best hotel is *Aipana Plaza*, at Praça Centro Civico 53 (tel. 224-4850).

You may want to enjoy the aerial views of Boa Vista, the river and the mountains in its vicinity. To arrange such a flight call tel. 224-5550. The Venezuelan consulate is at Rua Benjamin Constant 525, tel. 224-2182.

## On to Venezuela
Trucks set out for Venezuela from Rua Benjamin Constant, and one can try to catch a ride with them. A regular jeep service runs between Boa Vista and Ciudad Bolívar in Venezuela, and a bus sets out for Santa Elena every other day. Upon entering Venezuela, have your passport stamped at the border. Inquire at the Boa Vista police station where passports are stamped upon leaving Brazil.

# Benjamin Constant
This little town abuts the Colombian border and is a center of the drug trade. It is not a pleasant place to visit, and should be avoided if possible. It can be reached by boat from Manaus,

and is a stopover point en route to Colombia or Peru via Leticia. Two ferries a day travel between Benjamin Constant and Leticia (about a two-hour ride).

If you do decide to come here, take an excursion to the area of the rubber trees which produced an incredible economic boom in the Amazon area at the end of the last century.

## On to Colombia and Peru
Tabatinga is the Brazilian border town, lying close to Leticia in Colombia. Have your passport stamped in Tabatinga when leaving Brazil and again on your entry into Colombia at Leticia. Brazil's *Varig* Airlines flies twice weekly from Manaus to Iquitos in Peru, passing through Tabatinga on the way back. Entry visas into Peru are best obtained in Iquitos.

# Porto Velho
Porto Velho (pop. 220,000) is the capital of the State of Rondonia in the southern Amazon basin. It is the hub of an agricultural region whose main crops are rice, cocoa, and coffee. There are a number of Indian reservations in this area, where the tribes maintain a completely primitive way of life. Visiting these reservations is allowed only by special authorization from *Funai*, the agency reponsible for protecting and aiding the Indians.

Porto Velho is on the banks of Rio Madeira, and boats from Manaus reach its little port at irregular intervals. The town itself is not particularly interesting; it is a mere stopover station on the way to the Bolivian border.

Porto Velho offers a few mediocre hotels and a number of lower quality establishments. Of the restaurants, the *Almanara*, at José de Alencar 2624 is recommended. It is good, inexpensive and serves generous portions.

The airport, 7 km out of town, is served by regular flights from all over Brazil. Buses arrive from Manuas by a long and difficult road, passable only in the dry season. There is also a bus service from Cuiabá and Campo Grande to Porto Velho, and from Rio Branco in the west.

## On to Bolivia
Two buses a day leave Porto Velho for **Guajaramirim**, on the bank of the Rio Mamoré. Upon reaching this town on the Bolivian border be sure to get a Brazilian departure stamp in your passport. Ferries cross the river to **Guayaramerin**, on the Bolivian side, where you will receive an entry stamp, valid for a 30-day stay. Buses head from Guayaramerin to Riveralta,

*Crossing the river*

on the Rio Beni. Riveralta has air connections to Cochabamba and La Paz. Those who wish can continue upriver; riverboats proceed as far as Rurrenabaque.

# The Midwest

The Brazilian Midwest includes the states of Goiás, Mato Grosso, and Mato Grosso do Sul, as well as the federal district set aside for the new capital, Brasília.

This is one of Brazil's most remote, isolated regions. Until the end of the previous century, the journey from the Atlantic coast to Cuiaba entailed a long, arduous trek through Uruguay and northward up the Rio de la Plata! With the establishment of the new inland capital, the overland connections with the coastal region were greatly improved. New roads were paved, railroads were built, and cities were developed and modernized. The weather in the area is hot the year round.

## Brasília

The city of Brasília was established and proclaimed the Republic's formal and political capital on April 21, 1960, by the then-President of Brazil, Juscelino Kubitschek. Brasília unlike other cities which grow naturally with their populations, was developed in an artificial way. Built in the middle of nowhere, it was meant to attract the population of the crowded coastal strip to Brazil's interior. Brasília has an ultra-modern urban layout designed by Lucio Costa. Many of Brasília's buildings were designed by the famous architect Oscar Niemeyer.

The city was well planned and was built systematically. From overhead, it has a shape like an airplane. Its "wings" are the residential neighborhoods. Each of them, called a Super-Quadra, provides complete public services — schools, medical centers, churches, gas stations etc. The Super-Quadras are linked by boulevards. A superhighway traverses the length of the "fuselage", with the city's major public buildings arrayed alongside. The "tail" contains the national theater, sports stadium, and a shared train and bus terminal (*Rodoferroviária*). In the "cockpit" are the government buildings and Parliament. The city's "nose cone" abuts an artificial lake. There are also two diplomatic sectors (see "What to see") and two hotel districts (see "Where to stay"). Roads and neighborhoods are marked by numbers, not names.

Brasília lies 1200 m above sea level on a hot, dry plain covered in savannah vegetation. The population currently stands at 1,500,000. The idea of transforming Brazil's desolate central and western provinces into a center of culture and settlement has, in the main, been a failure. Morever, Brasília itself, meant to be the lodestone, has not lived up to expectations.

Area code: 061

## How to get there
Brasília's modern and convenient international airport is 12 km out of town. It has connections with all South American capitals plus New York, Miami, Los Angeles, and several European capitals. A shuttle service connects Brasília and Rio, and there are many daily flights to all of Brazil's major cities. Taxis run from the airport to town (rates are determined by meter), and a convenient bus reaches the *rodoviária* in the city center.

The combined bus terminal and train depot (called the *rodoferroviária*) is not to be confused with the *rodoviária* downtown, which accommodates the local and regional buses.

Buses leave from the *rodoferroviária* for all parts of Brazil: to Rio (20 hours or more), São Paulo (about 15 hours), and Bélem (about 40 hours). There is also bus service to Porto Velho, Cuiabá, and Campo Grande.

The railroad to Brasília was completed in 1981, and there is a line to São Paulo. The train ride is quite, comfortable and very inexpensive.

Area code: 061

## Where to stay
Almost all of Brasília's hotels are in two districts: Setor Hoteleiro Norte (the northern sector) and Setor Hoteleiro Sul (the southern sector). Hotel rates are 20% lower on weekends.

*HORSA Nacional*: SHS Quadra 01, Bloco "A"; tel. 321-7575, fax 223-9213.
*Carlton*: SHS Quadra 05, Bloco "G"; tel. 224-8819, fax 226-8109.
*Bristol*: SHS Quadra 04, Bloco "F"; tel. 321-6162. Moderate.
*Diplomat*: SHN Quadra 2, Bloco "L"; tel. 225-2010. Medium cost.
*El Pilar*: SHN Quadra 3, Bloco "F"; tel. 224-5915. Inexpensive.
*Brasília Imperial*: SHS Quadra 03, Bloco "E", "F", "H"; tel. 321-8747.
*Planalto*: SHS Quadra 03, Bloco "A"; tel. 225-6860.

Brasília itself has no cheap hotels. However, in Taguatinga, 30 minutes away, there are many such hotels.

## Where to eat
All the large hotels have restaurants, most serving continental cuisine. In the streets you can find many restaurants, but not so sophisticated like in Rio or São Paulo.

*Gaf:* Setor Habitaçoes Individuais Sul, Bloco C; tel. 248-1754. Closed on Sundays. One of the best in town.
*La Chaumiere:* Comercio Local Sul, Quadra 408, Bloco A; tel. 242-7599. Closed on Mondays. French cuisine.
*China:* Comercio Local Sul, Quadra 103, Bloco D; tel. 224-3339. Chinese.
*A Caminho do Natural:* Comercio Local Norte, Quadra 302, Bloco B; tel. 226-6733. Natural, self-service buffet. Closed on Sundays.

## Tourist services
There are tourist offices in the airport and at the *rodoferroviária*. Many travel agencies (including several with offices at the airport) offer organized tours of Brasília. This is a good, convenient way of getting to know the city.

**Rent-a-car:** The two largest companies are *Avis* (tel. 225-3975) and *Nobre* (tel. 246-6728).

## What to see
Start with an overview of the city from the **Torre de TV**, situated in the middle of the broad boulevard between the two wings of the "airplane". From here we see the city's basic structure, some of its important and modern buildings, and its layout of wide boulevards and highways.

Now head south, toward the front of the "airplane". Pass the *rodoviária* en route to downtown and stop at the **City Cathedral**, a modern structure and a famous Brasília landmark. From the outside the cathedral looks small. Upon entering, however, we find that most of it is underground. Statues of angels "soar" over the worshippers' heads in the cavernous hall.

On the eastern side of the broad boulevard is the **Teatro Nacional** (National Theater). Continuing along the boulevard, notice a series of rectangular buildings along the two sides. Each houses a government ministry. The last building on the right is the home of the Ministry of Foreign Affairs, the **Palacio do Itamarati**. It bears the name of the Ministry's former residence in Rio de Janeiro. This magnificent building is one of the most

## *BRASÍLIA*

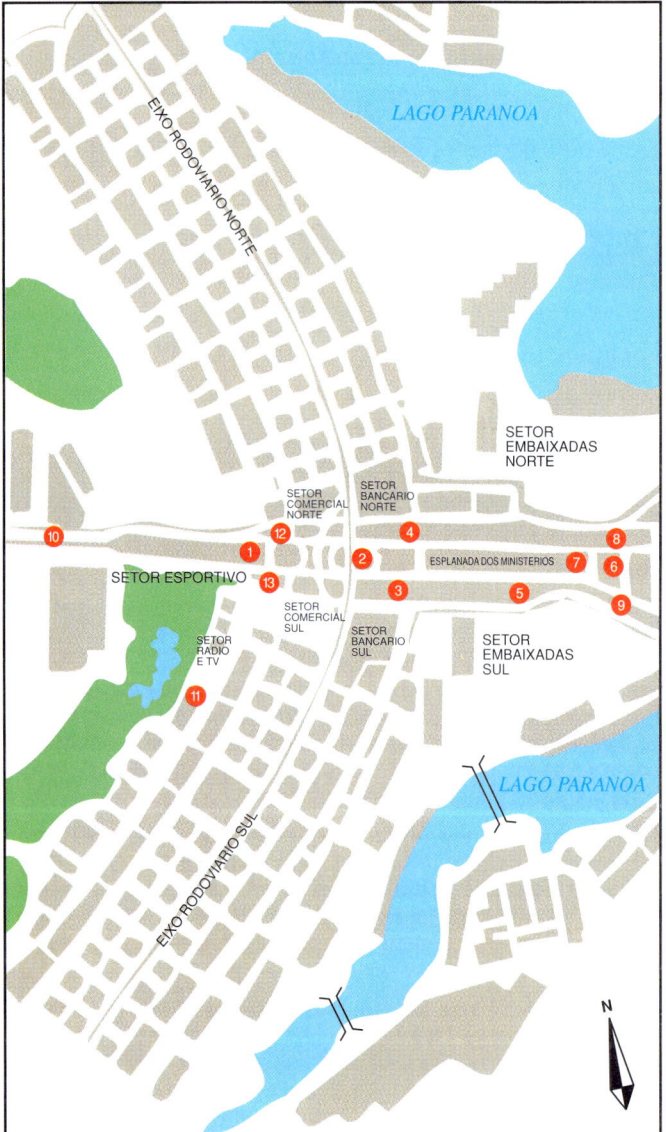

*The twin towers of House of Representatives*

impressive and beautiful in Brasília, with artificial waterfalls and pools (open Tues.-Fri. 10am-4pm. Be sure to ask the guards for permission to enter).

The cross-town boulevard ends at **Praça dos Tres Poderes** ("Three Powers Square"), a large, open square. Here you can see the complex which houses the country's three governmental authorities. The first structure is the **House of Representatives** — twin towers housing the offices of congressmen and senators. Semispherical buildings appear on either side of the towers; these are the assembly halls of the Senate and the Congress (open to visitors Tues.-Fri. 9am-noon, 2-5pm; weekends 2-5pm). The second edifice is the **Palacio do Planalto** (Presidential Palace) where the President has his offices (open Fri. 9-11am, 2-5pm). The third building is the **Supremo Tribunal Federal** (Supreme Court), and the statue opposite symbolizes blind justice. To enter, one needs permission from the guards and one has to be properly dressed. In the center of the square is the **city museum** of Brasília, and at the far end a large Brazilian national flag flutters in the breeze.

The street branching off the square in the direction from which we came leads to the grand **Palacio do Alvorador** (presidential residence) on the lake.

The two districts beyond the government ministries accommodate the **Setores Embaixadas** (diplomatic sectors). Each country with diplomatic representation in Brazil was apportioned a parcel of land and was asked to build an embassy in its best architectural tradition. In a few cases, the results are interesting and beautiful. The bridges crossing the lake at the front of the "airplane" lead to a quarter of luxurious villas where the city's wealthy class and the government ministers live. By observing how luxuriously the government ministers and officials live, one gets an impression of the enormous gap between rich and poor, which lies at the root of Brazil's serious social and economic predicament.

North of the main boulevard, in the rear part of the "body of the plane", is **Monumento Juscelino Kubitschek**, commemorating Brazil's late president and the founder of its new capital. The site includes a museum marking events in his life (open Tues.-Fri, 9am-noon and 1-6pm; weekends and holidays 9am-7pm.)

Continue a little further north along the boulevard until you reach a cross which marks the cornerstone of the city. To the right is the **Quartel General do Exercito** (army headquarters). Opposite it is a large statue shaped like an upside-down trigger. The statue's acoustic design is such that a rapidly repeated echo is heard at its center.

In the southern residential area, Quadra 702, is **Igreja Dom Bosco**. The church's blue glass creates wonderful light effects, and there is an immense chandelier hanging from the ceiling.

### Important Addresses
U.S. Embassy: SES, Avenida das Nacoes, Lote 3 (tel. 223-0120).
British Embassy: SES, Avenida das Nacoes, Lote 8 (tel. 225-2710).
Post Office: SCS, Edificio Nordeste.

# Goiânia
This youthful modern city, capital of the State of Goiás, is

210 km southeast of Brasília. Founded in October, 1933, it has a population of near a million inhabitants. The well-planned city is crisscrossed by wide, green boulevards. The buildings downtown, tall and modern, accommodate most of the commercial life in the state of Goiás.

In the center of the city is a spacious square called **Centro Civico**. The governor's mansion, **Palacio do Governo**, is situated here, and on Sunday mornings an artesania market takes place here. Avenida Araguaia, branching off the square, leads to **Parque Mutirama**, a spacious, green, park with a modest zoo and playgounds.

The airport is close to town, and regular flights land from all of Brazil's major cities. Buses reach the city terminal from Brasília, Cuiabá, Rio de Janeiro, and São Paulo.

## The Pantanal

The vast Pantanal area covers 230,000 sq/km of the Brazilian Midwest, in the area of the border with Bolivia and Uruguay. *Pantanal* means "large swamp", and the whole area is indeed covered from horizon to horizon with endless swamps — a garden of Eden for water plants and animals.

The Pantanal is the catchment area of Rio Paraguay and is crossed by many tributaries. Between June and September the water level in the marshes and rivers is low, and this is the best time to visit here. Much of the region is accessible by jeep during this season, permitting a close-up look at the abundant wildlife. Between October and March the rivers flood their banks, the water in the marshes rises, and access to animals becomes difficult. It is, however, the right time of year for botany lovers.

The diversity of wildlife in the area is immense and many rare species are found here in abundance: hundreds of species of birds and parrots in huge flocks, innumerable crocodiles (*jacarç*), herds of *kapibara* (the largest member of the rodent family), anaconda snakes, communities of monkeys, and more. These creatures share a tangle of marsh vegetation, bushes, and giant trees. Fish abound here too, making Pantanal one of the world's best spots for amateur fishing. The law permits catches of up to 30 kg per person.

The Pantanal is not "touristy" and is often left off itineraries to Brazil. Nevertheless, nature lovers will find it one of the most fascinating places in Brazil, or elsewhere.

One can reach the Pantanal from several points of departure:

from Corumbá (see "Corumbá") to the southwest, at the border crossing with Bolivia; from Campo Grande (see "Campo Grande"), and from Coxim, halfway between Campo Grande and Cuiaba. The most suitable section of Pantanal for touring is the northern region, which is easily reached from Cuiabá (see "Cuiabá").

# Cuiabá

Cuiabá (pop. 330,000) is the capital of the state of Mato Grosso. Rapid development in recent years has turned it into a modern, busy city, serving Western Brazil as a large commercial and industrial center. The vicinity of Cuiabá has several nature sites, rich in wildlife, of which the Pantanal is the most important and fascinating. In town, visit the large Gothic-style church known as **Igreja Bom Despache**.

Area code: 065

## How to get there

The airport is 12 km from downtown Cuiabá and is served regularly by *Varig*, *VASP*, and *Trans-Brazil*.

The bus terminal is 3 km from the city center. Many buses set out every day for Campo Grande, Brasília, São Paulo, and Rio de Janeiro. There are direct buses to Manaus and the journey takes several days, depending on the season and the condition of the road.

## Food and lodging

*Hotel Aurea Palace*: Rua Gen. Mello 63; tel. 322-2277. One of the best, all the facilities included.
*Eldorado Cuiabá*: Av. Isaac Povoas 1000; tel. 624-4000, fax 624-1480. New hotel with very high standards.
*Excelsior*: Av. Getúlio Vargas 264; tel. 322-6322.
*Mato Grosso*: Rua Com. Costa 2522; tel. 321-9121. Small and nice.

*Internacional*, at Praça Antonio Correia 40, is a good fish restaurant. For good Oriental food, try *Baalbek* at Avenida Vargas 600. Both are quite expensive. On Avenida Isaac Povoas there are several inexpensive restaurants and bars. *Patotinha* is a very popular bar with the young, who throng there on weekends.

## Tourist services

The local tourist office, *Turimat*, is on the city's central square, Praça da República. The staff is very friendly and efficient. Apart

*Exploring the Pantanal*

from its other activities, *Turimat* runs a telephone information service (tel. 139). Another information office is located at the airport.

**Car rental:** The *Nobre* company (main office at Avenida Vargas 600; branch office at the airport) provides good service.

Several travel agencies in Cuiabá arrange tours of the Pantanal for one day or several days. Make sure that the tours do not leave a free day on the schedule. Without a vehicle and a guide, you will simply be marooned there, and the heat and mosquitoes will rule out any possibility of enjoyable leisure.

## Exploring the Pantanal

The northern section of the Pantanal is the best for touring. Set out from Cuiabá by bus to **Poconé**, 100 km away. There are two very inexpensive hotels here which provide good basic services. From Poconé a road heads south to **Porto Jofre** — only a few houses and an anchorage for riverboats.

A compressed dirt road, 145 km long, crosses the marshes. The road crosses 128 wooden bridges on route, and from every bridge one can see dozens of crocodiles. In the dry season the road is passable for all types of cars. **Pixaim** lies 66 km south of

Poconé, and has a relatively expensive hostel, a restaurant and a gas station.

There are no buses south of Poconé, which means that one must either rent a car in Cuiabá or try one's luck at hitchhiking. There isn't much traffic, but the drivers are generally helpful. Equip yourself with food, and be prepared for long hours of waiting.

The trans-Pantanal road ends at Porto Jofre, on the Rio Cuiabá. Close by is Fazenda Santa Rosa, which is an expensive place to stay. One can travel upriver to Corumbá on a cargo boat. The journey takes three days, but the boats do not have a frequent or regular departure schedule. Alternatively, one can return the way one came.

### Santo Antônio de Leverger
This is the beach of the Rio Cuiabá, an hour's ride from the city. Buses leave frequently for the beach from the *rodoviária* in Cuiabá. It is a lovely beach; the water is clean and good for swimming and fishing enthusiasts are attracted by the abundant fish.

Santo Antônio is best known as a Garden of Eden for bird watchers and nature lovers. The variety of birds nesting here is incredible — multitudes of birds of prey, parrots, toucans, and many other species.

## Campo Grande
Campo Grande (pop. 450,000) is the capital of the State of Mato Grosso do Sul. The overland route from the Brazilian coast to Corumbá and Bolivia passes through this city. The city, modern and quite pleasant, is the commercial hub of a bountiful agricultural hinterland, where the major crops are wheat and rice.

Downtown, at Barão do Rio Branca 1843, is **Museu Dom Bosco**, the Indian Museum, a truly worthwhile place to visit. It exhibits a rich collection of Indian implements from Mato Grosso, *artesania*, musical instruments, and a large collection of stuffed animals of the species inhabiting the Pantanal.

Campo Grande is a suitable point of departure for tours of the Pantanal area, although this entails a long ride to the periphery of the marshes. Tourists continuing onwards to Bolivia are better advised to set out from Corumbá.

Area code: 067

## How to get there

Campo Grande has regular air connections with Brazil's major cities, and *VASP* flies from here to Corumbá. A few buses a day arrive from São Paulo (a 14-hour ride), Rio de Janeiro, Brasília, and Cuiabá. Buses travel to Corumbá only in the dry season, because the road crosses a marshy area. Two trains make the trip between São Paulo and Corumba daily, passing through Campo Grande at 8am and at 8:30pm. The night train is expensive, because it consists of sleeping cars only. The beautiful ride to Corumbá lasts 11 hours. It is better to make the trip from São Paulo by bus as it is much faster than by train.

# Corumbá

Corumbá (pop. 85,000) is situated on the banks of the Rio Paraguay, close to the Bolivian border, on the edge of the Pantanal marshes. Because of its location, it is a good launching place for exploring the marshes. The town itself is quite placid, with mostly one or two story houses. A small port on the river caters mostly for fishing boats.

Of the several hotels in Corumbá, the best is the *Santa Monica*, an average quality establishment at Rua Coelho 345 (tel. 231-2481). The rest of the hotels provide basic services only, at low prices. Particularly low cost hotels are found on Rua Delamare.

The **tourist office**, *MS Tur* at Rua Dom Acuim 405, is efficient and helpful.

Area code: 067

## How to get there

Corumbá's small airport is very close to the city, and *VASP* has daily flights to and from Campo Grande and Cuiabá. Two trains a day reach Corumbá from São Paulo (a 35-hour trip) and from Campo Grande (about 12 hours). In the rainy season, the Pantanal marshes flood the road to Campo Grande, and only the train can get through.

Cargo boats ply the Rio Paraguay, crossing the Pantanal while heading north upriver to destinations close to Cuiabá. The cruise takes up to ten days, and in the dry season one can see abundant wildlife on the riverbanks.

## Excursions to the Pantanal

In the dry season, a short excursion in the Corumbá area will suffice to reach concentrations of wildlife. Access is far more difficult during the rainy season, when the rivers spill over their banks and flood the marshes.

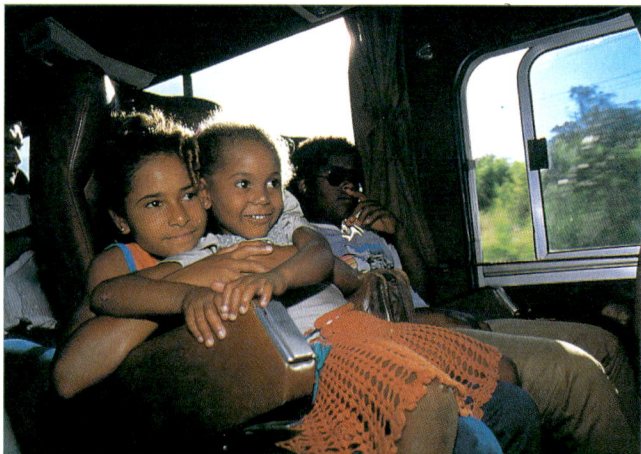

All travel agencies in the city offer boat trips to the Pantanal. The *Pantanal Express*, at Avenida General Rondon 1355, is recommended. Another possibility is to find a private guide in the small fishermen's harbor.

There are several hostels (*fazendas*) in the heart of the marsh area around Corumbá, and they can be used as points of departure for short outings. The best of them is *Fazenda Santa Clara*, about 120 km from Corumbá. Make inquiries in Corumbá (tel. 231-5797).

## On to Bolivia

When leaving Brazil be sure to have your passport stamped. Do this in Corumbá, at the police station in the train depot. Buses set out for the border from Praça da República every day, every half hour, 6am-6pm. Travelers with heavy loads are usually requested to ride in a special bus, which departs from the end of the adjacent Rua Antônio Mario.

On entering Bolivia, have your passport stamped at the border. The stamp allows for a 30-day stay. From the border, taxis set out for nearby **Puerto Suarez**, the Bolivian border town. From there, the famous "death train" leaves daily, making its way to Santa Cruz in about 20 hours. The train is so called because of the many delays on the way, sometimes hours long, and the stories told about its going off the tracks... There are twice-weekly flights to Santa Cruz and La Paz.

Although by Brazilian standards, the Brazilian side of the border zone is not a particularly well developed or orderly area, the change between it and Bolivia is nevertheless dramatic. One feels it in the Puerto Suarez train station and on the train, which is packed with Indians and their belongings.

## Currency exchange

Because the exchange rates for Bolivian currency are better in Corumbá than over the border in Bolivia itself, change at least enough money to last until Santa Cruz or La Paz. For buying Brazilian currency, however, this area is at a disadvantage. Moneychangers congregate on Rua Antônio Maria, and there is a branch of Banco de Brasil at Rua de Jungo 13.

# *I*NDEX

# *INDEX*

# *I*<small>NDEX</small>

# NOTES

# NOTES

# NOTES

# NOTES

# NOTES

# NOTES

# NOTES

# NOTES

Fuck off

# QUESTIONNAIRE

In our efforts to keep up with the pace and pulse of Brazil, we kindly ask your cooperation in sharing with us any information which you may have as well as your comments. We would greatly appreciate your completing and returning the following questionnaire. Feel free to add additional pages.

Our many thanks!

---

To: Inbal Travel Information (1983) Ltd.
18 Hayetzira Street
Ramat Gan 52521
Israel

Name: _____

Address: _____

_____

Occupation: _____

Date of visit: _____

_____

Purpose of trip (vacation, business, etc.): _____

_____

_____

Comments / Information: _____

_____

_____

_____

_____

_____

_____

_____

_____

_____

_____

_____

**INBAL Travel Information Ltd.**
P.O.B. 39090 Tel Aviv
ISRAEL 61390